PTF58

Islands of Promise

Philippe Vallette and Christine Causse

Islands of Promise

Photographs by Alexis Rosenfeld
Maps by Jean-Pierre Magnier

Preface by Isabelle Autissier

Translated from French by John Tittensor

ACTES SUD - NAUSICAÁ - MARE NOSTRUM

Contents

History unfolds on an island-planet. A tiny island-planet – ours – in the midst of a vast universe containing billions and billions of "celestial bodies", all similar yet all different. This one is set apart from the others by the water that covers three quarters of its surface, marking out not just those big islands so pompously termed "continents" by their inhabitants, but small ones as well: hundreds, thousands, maybe tens of thousands of them. Just how many we don't really know, since the word "island" can mean so many things: a place surrounded by water, of course, but is that all? Is a rock measuring a few square metres an island? Is Australia an island? Ultimately, what's the point of having invented the word if we don't know how to use it properly?

Put the question to any author or scriptwriter: they'll tell you an island is a place of dreams and imaginings. A scientist will go on about endemic species and remarkable, fragile biodiversity. A sailor will see a promising landfall or a navigation danger. A general will hector you with geostrategy, an economist will lecture you about tourist development, transport costs or energy availability. A banker will hint discreetly at tax havens, and the man in the street will bore you stiff with his last holidays. And they might all be referring to the same place.

So is there any sense in trying to pin islands down in a book? Is it actually possible to inventory them, classify them, draw up lists of resemblances and equivalences, come to more broadly applicable conclusions about their history, situation and evolution? What point is there in comparing Kerguelen with Singapore, Ouessant with Malta, the rocky Minquiers off Jersey with Greenland? And yet, apart from the fact that they are all "islands", aren't there good reasons for thinking they can make their own very specific contribution to the evolution of the world? And if so, what's their common denominator?

An island is first of all a self-contained territory whose contour you can run your finger over on a map. It's an inside and an outside, whose outline forms a separation between a world of here and now and – maybe – other worlds far away over the dark sea. The warm welcome sailors get from most islanders is a sign of gratitude to those who have braved the ocean to make the encounter possible. And so the island, which demands voyaging, speaks of receptivity, journeys, discoveries, contacts and intermingling.

But it is also an entity in its own right. The more isolated it is, the more it develops its own special character, its environment, its laws and languages. Imagine the sheer chance involved when a seed crosses the Southern Ocean then washes up – and germinates – on Kerguelen. Then imagine the tens of thousands of years of its solitary evolution, its gradual adaptation to local conditions. And are we aware that the Guanches, the vanished original people of the Canary Islands, lived for centuries without contact with other civilisations?

What does it matter to an island that other places exist? For it is self-sufficient, either in its starkness or its profusion.

The island as a world in itself: that's the fantasy shared by so many of us. Every Robinson Crusoe climbing to the highest point on his island is just as awed by his isolation as he is delighted by the discovery of a territory, a kingdom at his feet. To our eyes wearied by the complexity of the world, the island seems manageable, a place for fulfilling dreams of a different relationship with nature, of a different social order. Then we let our mind wander through notions of noble savages, complete liberty or, on the contrary, an existence guided by strict principles elevated to universal status. And each time the island keeps its promises: restoring our power to act and let our imagination run free.

Yet however isolated they may be, today's islands cannot escape globalisation. Pierre Premier – the rock located at latitude 69° South where my boat was only the third ever to make landfall – is now caught up in the turmoil of global warming. Who can say that one day an offshore oil pumping relay won't be built there?

In a context of standardisation – or outright homogenisation – of the world's societies, the margins are always interesting: for it's there that, often unknown or ignored, utopian practices endure which will have their part to play in helping to solve our globalised problems. For farming solutions, for example, are we not currently turning as much to ancient crop varieties as to the genetic modification laboratories?

Global warming, the collapse of biodiversity, the end of oil, the breakdown of social bonds, lawlessness, forced migrations, pollution and so on: our planet's dominant model is at the end of its rope and now a source of more problems than answers. The concept of the sole, radically centralised frame of reference is breaking apart before our very eyes. The Internet means more and more sharing, energy is now available in a host of forms for which we shall soon be as much producers as consumers, and agriculture is timidly tip-toeing towards our cities and sometimes finding a foothold in their very centres.

Building the future now means doing everything possible to coordinate our thinking and our energy around an approach that amounts to more than just pointlessly papering over the cracks in the existing system. And it's here that islands are rediscovering their natural, rightful place at the heart of things. Directly confronted with all kinds of difficulties, they lack the scale and the capacity for concealment: their problems, with their roots and ramifications, are out there on full display, like mirrors held up to the oblivious or blind continents.

Are islands signalling what awaits us? No question. For these marginal parts of the world are also home to the seeds of change, to empirical or revolutionary solutions. Hot or cold, big or small, close or distant, overpopulated or deserted, pristine or devastated – what islands have in common is their status as finite territorial entities open to experimental ventures.

So let's go out and get acquainted with them; and let's consider the possibility that in addition to their individual virtues, they have a far-reaching message for us. The future no longer belongs to the consumerist/Taylorist model, with its manufacturing and farming whose output has to be transported at immense expense, over enormous distances, and at the cost of an inadmissible carbon footprint. Our future can only be built on steadily increasing localness and interactivity. Trends in farming, energy, skills and social organisation mean our twenty-first century is going to go over to networking: we will be simultaneously producers and consumers of goods and services redefined in terms of their ability to find their niche in an ecologically acceptable cycle. Not only will our planet cease to be no more than a handful of continents surrounded by satellite islands, it will become an archipelago of interchange, with each community achieving greater autonomy at the same time as its external relations proliferate.

Sources of inspiration, models of civilisation: there is so much we urgently need to discover, admire, understand and draw on in this ocean-borne scattering of confetti – the world's islands.

ISABELLE AUTISSIER

Island Dreaming

Islands: these sprinklings of earth over the immensity of the Ocean have always triggered flights of fancy. In the collective imagination they are synonymous with adventure, freedom and solitude. They are the landfall at the end of the voyage, the place where you get away from it all, the sweet life, paradise on earth. But they are, too, lands of the future, of unlimited possibility, of tomorrow's emergent opportunities. Faced with today's upheavals island-dwellers, the first to be confronted with the changes affecting our planet, are coming up with the necessary solutions for a more liveable, more equitable world.

Seen from the sky, the Earth yields all its beauty: ochre expanses of desert where a dirt road or an earth-coloured village can just be made out, snow-capped peaks playing hide and seek with the clouds, the mystery of tropical forests stretching away out of site. And, of course, the sea: infinity, the void, eternity – until, that is, an island appears.

Minuscule and remote, like some great ship that has strayed far from land and been left to the mercy of the currents, it gleams in the sun with its foam-edged shores and pellucid, suddenly depthless lagoons. Under the play of wind and light the blue of the Ocean alters and shifts in countless hues from green to turquoise to sky blue, ice blue, cobalt, ultramarine, indigo, Persian blue, azure, cyan and aquamarine.

Whether under the tropics or in the glacial waters of the end of the world, islands are a haven of life, an oasis in what seems a watery desert. Sometimes a broken-off scrap of a continent, floating free for millions of years, or a molten mass risen out of the waves during those monstrous tremors that shake the earth's entrails. Or perhaps the long, patient work of the tiny marine organisms called coral. And as time passes, islands change: each year new ones are born, while others vanish beneath the surface. Isolated and encompassed by water, down the centuries they have been colonised by a host of different plants and animals. Seeds, larvae and eggs brought by wind and waves washed up on the shore. Sometimes larger creatures arrived after a long journey spent clinging to some fortuitous raft, then adapted and evolved. Cut off in the midst of the Ocean, the fragments of land they lived on saw the emergence of unique, living communities.

But the greatest asset islands can boast is the incredible diversity of their populations. Some have been inhabited since the dawn of humanity, others were colonised down the ages by people who came in boats from distant continents, bringing with them seeds, animals and plants which sometimes thrived on their new territories.

Little by little, then, islands change, with their history and individual character taking shape as time goes by.
And so each island is irreplaceable: unique, singular, precious, home to peoples, cultures, landscapes, flora and fauna to be found nowhere else. This diversity is part of islands' contribution to the world's wealth.
Yet while islands conjure up visions of paradise and untrammelled freedom, and of places of refuge far from the continent and its madding crowds, the reality for their inhabitants is quite different. Even when markedly dissimilar in terms of their history and their strengths and weaknesses, they have a number of shared problems to cope with: more than other parts of the world, they are facing an unprecedented environmental upheaval. Small and surrounded by water, they have been hit very hard by global warming and its chain of consequences for the weather, the Ocean, fresh water, and animal and plant life. Moreover, the undermining of biodiversity both marine and terrestrial weighs increasingly heavily on these small states where such basic resources are crucial to social and economic development.
All of which means that islands represent a primary interface with today's global issues. As the first to register the undeniable changes in their living environment, they are also the first to have to take emergency measures against salinization of their drinking water, protect their shoreline against rising sea levels, minimise soil loss due to erosion and preserve their marine ecosystems.
Should islands, then, be considered as sentinels? Or as environmental laboratories? Among the first land areas to feel the impact of environmental change, they are consequently the places where the effects of counter-measures can be most quickly assessed: small-scale programs are easier to implement and the environment reacts that much more rapidly. As Kiribati Islands president Anote Tong has emphasised, "Climate change affects all nations of this planet, but in varying degrees. The irony, however, is that it is the poorest and the smallest countries with the least contribution of greenhouse gases which are paying the ultimate price, in order that the lifestyles and development agendas of some countries may be maintained."[1]
Environmental disruption now affects us all, which is why we all have to take steps. As the Millennium Ecosystem Assessment Report for 2005 warned, "If we fail to acknowledge our debt [to nature] and fail to prevent it from increasing, we will be jeopardising the dreams of people all over the world regarding freedom from hunger, extreme poverty and avoidable disease; at the same time we will be increasing the danger of sudden changes to life-enabling systems, changes against which not even the wealthiest will be protected." Debate about our societies, our lifestyles and the changes impacting our planet may make it possible to modify current trends with a view to preserving the resources and natural environments we depend on. Islands, which are showing us the way and coming up with the answers, will help all of us to take up today's challenges and ensure a worthwhile future for our children.

FACING PAGE: THIS YOUNG VEZO FISHERMAN FROM SOUTHERN MADAGASCAR KNOWS THAT HIS SURVIVAL HINGES ON THE OCEAN AND THE COMPLEX EQUILIBRIUM BETWEEN HUMAN ACTIVITIES AND PRESERVATION OF THE NATURAL ENVIRONMENT.

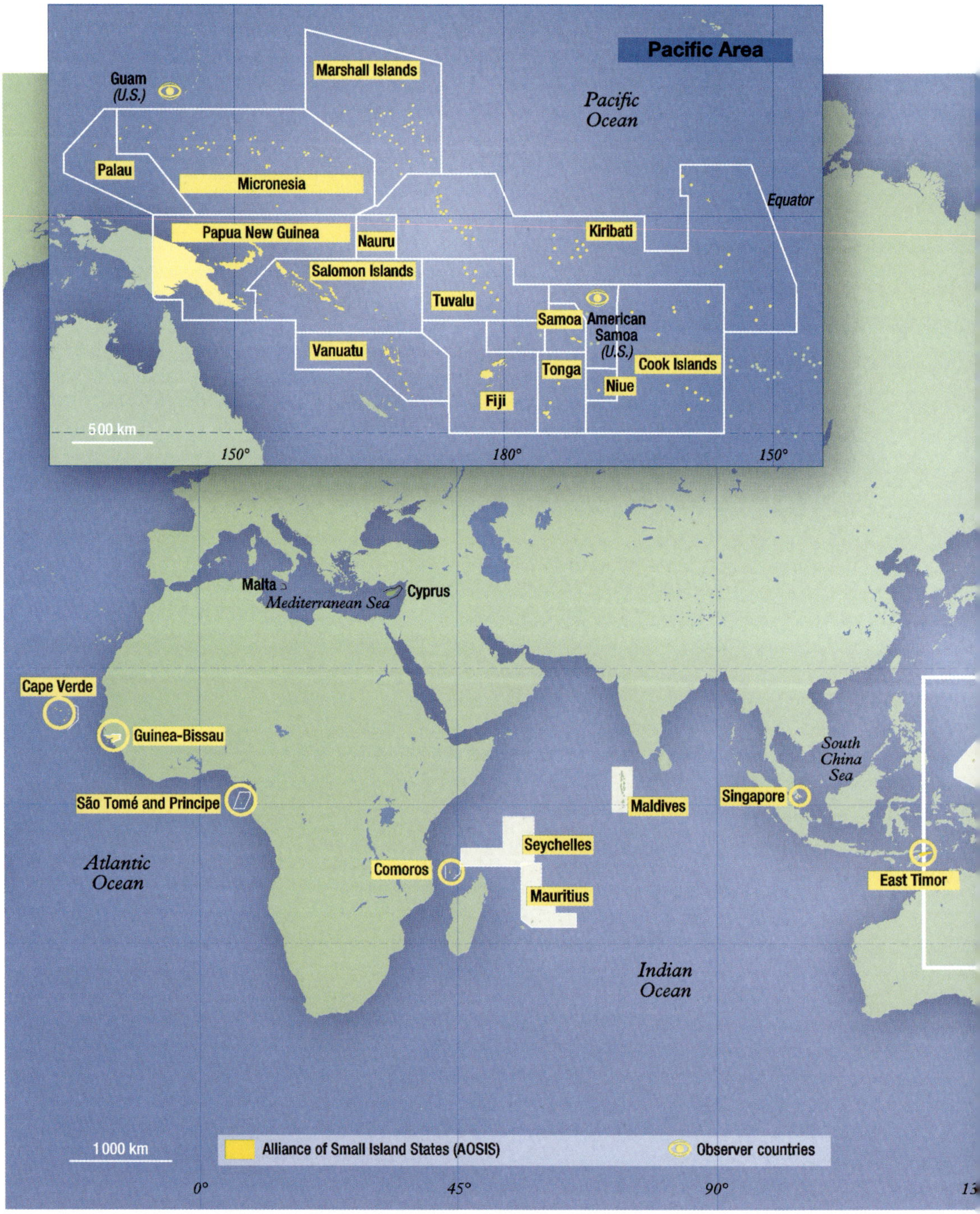

ALLIANCE OF SMALL ISLAND DEVELOPING STATES.

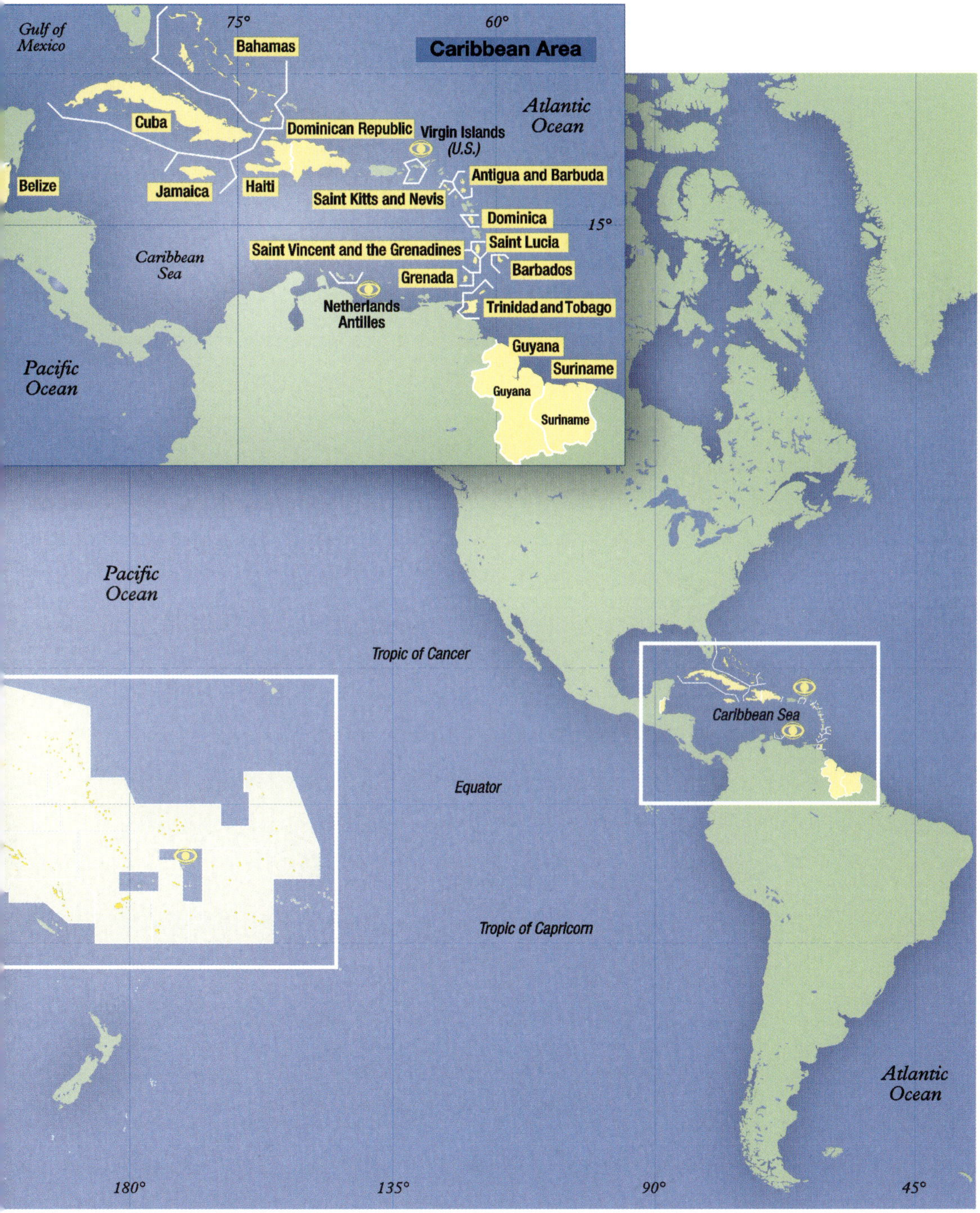
Caribbean Area
Gulf of Mexico
75°
60°
Bahamas
Atlantic Ocean
Cuba
Dominican Republic
Virgin Islands (U.S.)
Belize
Jamaica
Haiti
Antigua and Barbuda
Saint Kitts and Nevis
Dominica
15°
Saint Vincent and the Grenadines
Saint Lucia
Caribbean Sea
Grenada
Barbados
Netherlands Antilles
Trinidad and Tobago
Guyana
Suriname
Pacific Ocean
Guyana
Suriname
Pacific Ocean
Tropic of Cancer
Caribbean Sea
Equator
Tropic of Capricorn
Atlantic Ocean
180°
135°
90°
45°

What is an Island?

An island for taking refuge, for hiding, for dreaming, for living… A faraway island, an island on the horizon, an island paradise… A prison island, a solitude island, a nightmare island. An island for being alone, for tasting peace and finding unity with nature. All these islands people our collective imagination. But what is an island exactly? Does a lump of coral with a single palm tree share the same essence as the wild immensity of Greenland? We all have our own clear idea of the entity called "island", but in fact the term covers many different realities – while at the same time all islands share certain common features.

ISLANDS OF THE WORLD

LAND SURROUNDED BY WATER

For most of us an island is a small piece of land surrounded by water. For geographers the term designates a piece of land separated from the nearest continent by at least two kilometres of water. Its area can extend from 0.15 to two million square kilometres, the biggest island of all being Greenland; so an island can be a mere rock with no fresh water, or a land mass including very different landscapes and environments. Our planet is home to some 175,000 islands – excluding the island continents of Australia and Antarctica – which total 1.86% of the earth's surface and 7% of its visible land mass. Inventorying them, though, is problematical: some are of continental, volcanic or reef-based origin, some are flat and barely rise above the surface of the sea, and some are mountainous. Then there are the ephemeral ones: barrier islands – made up of accumulated soil or sand and separated from a continent only by a lagoon or an estuary – have their shape and area modified over time by currents, tides and variations in sea level. In 2001 scientists listed 1,492 of them, but ten years later a new study using satellite images and topographical and marine maps added 657 more, for a total of 2,149.

Only 9,000 of the world's islands are inhabited. A worldwide tendency is for human communities to settle near coastlines and today more than half our planet's population has made this choice, with the proportion increasing steadily. This makes islands conducive to major population concentrations, and in spite of representing only 7% of available land, they are home to 600 million people, or almost one person in every ten. If we add in their marine territory – what is known as the

PREVIOUS DOUBLE PAGE: ISLANDS ARE TO BE FOUND IN ALL THE WORLD'S SEAS, BUT THE GREAT MAJORITY OF INDEPENDENT ISLAND STATES ARE IN THE TROPICAL REGIONS.

FOLLOWING DOUBLE PAGE: ISLANDS CAN BE OF VOLCANIC, CONTINENTAL OR CORAL ORIGIN, BUT SOME ARE NO MORE THAN SHORT-LIVED SANDBANKS.

"exclusive economic zone" (EEZ) – they represent in all a sixth of the earth's surface. Which gives them considerable economic and social significance, despite being so often forgotten or neglected in relation to the continents.

THE ISLAND: A MULTI-FACETED ENTITY

Being multi-faceted, the island does not lend itself to simplistic analysis. As geographer/island specialist Louis Brigand[2] emphasises, "The island is indeed a territory surrounded by water, but to this definition we have to add a host of very different situations. There's also the notion of isolation that can be applied to the island or, more exactly, to the concept of insularity. You could say that Australia is an island, and the Earth an island in the universe. I see size and the relationships with the coastline as very important. An island you can walk around in one day is probably more 'island' than another. And the fact that you can take it in in a single look also counts. In Jules Verne's *The Mysterious Island* the explorers reach the top of the mountain and discover that they are on an island because they can observe it at a glance in its entirety. It's crucial to be able to grasp an island on a human scale, in terms of walking and time. For me, the smaller the island, the more 'island' it is. It really amuses people when I say I'm an island specialist; it doesn't seem really serious – it makes people think of holidays, the sun, a certain kind of lifestyle, a low-key world where you live the good, free life. People's initial reaction to islands is very positive, but it also reflects a very rosy view of things. The reality is quite different, of course."
But islands do have a status all their own. Sought out for their isolation, they encourage spirituality, and some have become places of withdrawal from the world, complete with monasteries and other religious buildings. In the course of history they've also served as dumping grounds for marginal population groups: everywhere islands have been used for prisons, hospitals for infectious diseases, centres for difficult children and so on.

ISLANDS AS INSPIRATION FOR POETS, WRITERS AND MUSICIANS

The island is a world in miniature where dreams, fantasies, hopes, violence and solitude are more pronounced than elsewhere: a distant, extreme shut-in world that fires the imagination. It is hardly surprising that islands have been such an inspiration for creative people. Poets, whether islanders or not, have sung their praises in every language, writers and filmmakers have found them remarkable settings for powerful plots: Robert Louis Stevenson's

Treasure Island (1883), for example, is a repair for pirates and the scene of thrilling adventures. And the island is also a perfect setting for raising philosophical issues. Its isolation can be synonymous with freedom, but also with imprisonment, and anguish for those washed up after a shipwreck or a plane crash, as in Daniel Defoe's *Robinson Crusoe* (1719), Jules Verne's *The Mysterious Island* (1874), William Golding's *Lord of the Flies* (1954), Robert Merle's *The Island* (1962) and Robert Zemeckis's film *Cast Away* (2000). In this situation a man without even the basic necessities has to fight for his survival, and finds himself confronted with his existential condition: how to remain a man when utterly alone, like Robinson Crusoe and the hero of *Cast Away*? Or how to rebuild a viable society out of a group of human beings in total isolation, like Golding's schoolboys or the mutineers of *The Island*, who have to begin a whole new life?

CROSSROADS AND MELTING POTS

THE FIRST INHABITANTS

Since the dawn of humanity, men have set out across the sea in search of new lands and new wealth. The islands closest to the continents were very quickly inhabited: during the last Ice Age – 18,000 years ago – the level of the sea was 120 metres lower than it is today, and some islands could even be reached on foot. Getting to Australia, for example, involved only the crossing of a few sounds. On the other hand, most of the Pacific islands were colonised by excellent mariners, the ancestors of today's Polynesians. This population process began around 3000 BCE and took place over thousands of years (see box, page 29). Other islands were inhabited much more recently: the Maoris moved to New Zealand only in the fourteenth century. The first inhabitants of the Pacific islands were long cut off from the rest of the world. Then improvements in navigation and boat building techniques brought the great powers of East and West to more distant shores where they traded in spices, wood, exotic materials, precious stones – and slaves. The Chinese, Arabs and Europeans set up trading posts and fought each other for control of territories lost in the middle of the ocean, often with tragic consequences for the native peoples involved.

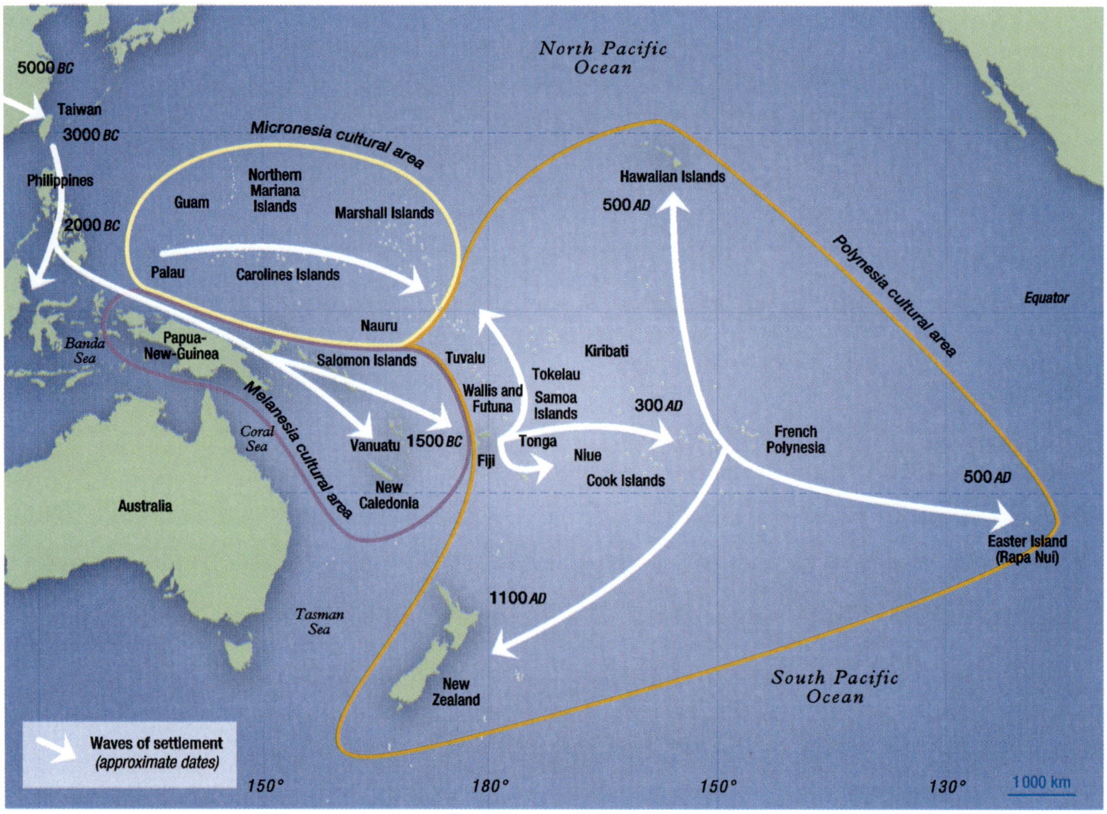

THE PACIFIC WAS CONQUERED BY PEOPLE IN OCEAN-GOING PIROGUES. AS EARLY AS 3000 BCE THE POLYNESIANS WERE COLONISING THESE ISLANDS ONE AFTER ANOTHER AS THEY EXTENDED THEIR INFLUENCE OVER AN ENORMOUS AREA.

THE GREAT PACIFIC ADVENTURE

The incredible adventure of populating the Pacific – the world's largest ocean – was spread over thousands of years. Some five millennia ago, and for reasons still unknown, the ancestors of the Polynesians set off in their pirogues from the Bismarck archipelago, near Papua New Guinea. Their sea-crossing probably involved two stages: a sortie by a small reconnaissance party in fast, easily manoeuvrable pirogues, followed by the rest of the community aboard boats capable of holding up to two hundred people, together with animals, seed plants, provisions and water. These later were probably catamarans driven by sails and oars.

Study of the Lapita culture, characterised by geometrically-adorned ceramics, has enabled us to reconstruct the itinerary of these first explorers. Heading west, they landed successively on the Solomon Islands (c. 1500 BCE), Fiji (c. 1240 BCE), and Tonga a century later. Polynesia was conquered at the beginning of the Christian era.

In 400 CE Polynesians, doubtless from the Marquesas, reached the island of Hawaii, 5,000 kilometres away. To prove that such a feat was possible, in 1976 American anthropologist Ben Finney made the Tahiti-Hawaii crossing in twenty-five days aboard the *Hokulea*, a replica of the early Polynesian boats. Peerless navigators, the Polynesians never let up in their colonisation of the Pacific. Some of them reached Easter Island in 500 CE, leaving over six hundred stone giants, four metres tall, along the coastline as testimony to these initial settlements. Other expeditions set out from the Society Islands towards New Zealand.

The settling of Micronesia in the North-Eastern Pacific is attributed to a community of potters – like the Lapita, but of a different culture – who are thought to have left the Philippines around 1500 BCE.

By about a thousand years ago, the entire Pacific had been conquered. Without maps, and with no means of calculating their course and speed, the Polynesians had crisscrossed the planet's vastest ocean, braving the elements with only their knowledge of the stars, sun, currents and weather to guide them.

EMIGRANTS, EXPLORERS, COLONISERS: SUCCESSIVE WAVES OF IMMIGRATION

"Land! Land ho!" Perched in the crow's nest atop the mainmast, the sailor pointed towards a spit of white sand fringed with coconut palms. The year was 1492 and Christopher Columbus, in search of a route to India, was about to berth in the Bahamas, in the Caribbean Sea. What he had discovered was not Asia, but America!

FOLLOWING DOUBLE PAGE: ISLANDS HAVE ALWAYS FIRED THE IMAGINATION: WITH THEIR SUMMONS TO TRAVEL AND ADVENTURE THEY CONJURE UP VISIONS OF SOLITUDE, FREEDOM AND GETTING AWAY FROM IT ALL.

A few years later, in 1497, Portuguese explorer Vasco da Gama was the first to open up the Spice Route in the Indian Ocean, after passing via the Cape of Good Hope, discovered by his compatriot Bartolomeu Dias ten years earlier. In the decades to come, other expeditions would follow, discovering new islands, India, and the remote regions of the Pacific, and returning laden with fabulous plants that quickly found favour with the nobles of Europe's courts: pepper and vanilla from Madagascar, cinnamon bark from Ceylon, cloves and nutmeg from the Moluccas. Thus began a merciless struggle between the great kingdoms bent on appropriating the riches of these isolated, exotic lands and establishing vast colonial empires. Coveted as much for their products as for their importance as sources of food for sailing ships, these islands passed from hand to hand in the course of clashes between the rival powers of the time. Dominica was one notable example: a verdant paradise situated north of Guadalupe, this West Indian island was peopled by Caribbean Indians when Columbus dropped anchor there in 1493.

The Spanish settlers would be supplanted by the English in 1627, and the English by the French in 1632. The English took over again in 1759, followed by the French in 1778 and the return of the English in 1783. After two further attempts by the French, the English succeeded in claiming the island definitively in 1814. With each new conflict the capital, Roseau, was razed by cannon and fires. In 1967 Dominica became an associated state of the United Kingdom, then declared its independence in 1978. On various desert islands passing sailors hunted, fished and cut wood. Settlements

IN SOUTHERN MADAGASCAR, A VEZO WOMAN RETURNS HOME WITH THE DAY'S CATCH.
FOR ISLAND DWELLERS THE OCEAN IS VITAL AND OMNIPRESENT.

sprang up and grew. Some of the islands' indigenous species failed to cope with these upheavals: the dodo, for example – a large, flightless bird from the island of Mauritius – disappeared in the late seventeenth century, after the destruction of the forests it lived in. Its extinction was hastened, too, by the rats and monkeys brought to the island by the Europeans, which robbed the dodos' nests.
Similarly the arrival of explorers on an inhabited island had dramatic consequences for the local communities, even when they were not reduced to slavery, shipped elsewhere against their will, driven off their land or subjected to forced labour in the settlers' plantations and mines. They were faced with new cultures and religious practices, as well as economic activities that radically altered their living environment. The colonists brought plants and animals that modified the landscape and its cultivation; they cleared, sowed and planted; they built schools, hospitals and churches; they developed irrigation systems and ways of transporting produce towards the coasts and ports, and then to other countries far across the sea, so that many tropical islands became enormous plantations of coconuts, sugar and bananas. All these changes would have irreversible effects on the future of these island communities.

PEOPLE AND CULTURES

ALL KINDS OF ETHNIC INFLUENCES

Today's island communities have their origins in a long history of waves of migration. Many of them are made up of descendants of the islands' original inhabitants, of the explorers from Europe, Asia or Africa, and in some cases of slaves brought in by settlers to work on the land or in mines. The outcome is a complex ethnic mix: "Islands are crossroads for civilisations," comments specialist Louis Brigand. "Despite their isolation, they are transit points where people meet and mix. On the island of Reunion, for example, communities speaking different languages and practising different religious coexist with no major clashes."
As a result of successive occupations, island cultures have changed: certain traditional and religious features have been abandoned – sometimes willingly, sometimes under pressure – and social life has been changed and enriched by different influences. The Republic of Palau, a small Micronesian state in the Pacific, to the east of the Philippines, has undergone repeated invasions. Comprising over 250 islands with a total of 20,000 inhabitants, it was most likely first populated more than 3,000 years ago by people arriving from the Philippines in big sailing pirogues. Now it is home to communities of Malay, Melanesian, Filipino and Polynesian origin, but has also been marked in linguistic, cultural and religious terms by a series of colonial episodes: after being claimed by, respectively, Britain, Spain, Germany and Japan, it remained an American protectorate until independence finally came

FOLLOWING DOUBLE PAGE: SINCE ANCIENT TIMES PEOPLE HAVE NAVIGATED FROM ISLAND TO ISLAND ALONG THE WELCOMING SHORES OF THE MEDITERRANEAN, BUILDING CITIES FOUNDED ON TRADE AND FISHING, AS IN SCIACCA, SICILY.

in 1994. Palauan and English are the two official languages, but people also speak Japanese, Filipino, Angaur on the island of Angaur and Sonsorolese on the island of Sonsorol. The principal religions are Christianity and *modekngei*, a specifically Palauan faith founded in 1915 which mixes Christian beliefs and ancient traditional practices. The favourite sport is baseball, introduced by – surprisingly – the Japanese, during their occupation of Palau from 1914 to 1944.

"Not only do island communities muster a rich diversity of cultural characteristics," Louis Brigand continues, "they have also demonstrated their ability to give birth to new cultural forms. They are conducive to creativity and introspection, as can be seen, for example in traditional music. Islands are the great source of musical innovation, for example: think of places like Cuba, Jamaica, Cap Verde and everywhere in the Caribbean."

Unfortunately traditional forms of knowledge are in the process of disappearing as islanders adopt modern lifestyles and consumption habits. Globalisation and tourism tend to erase cultural specificities, although for Louis Brigand the news is not all bad: "This is happening in the islands of Brittany, for instance. But there are also grounds for seeing a revival, as island territories become more appreciated for what they are. There's a sense of community among their inhabitants and it's not uncommon that island residents choose another island for their holidays. When one island dweller

TRADITIONAL BOAT-BUILDING TOOLS AND TECHNIQUES LIVE ON IN ISLAND CULTURES.

meets another, something special happens. Since 2011 France's 'Les Insulaires' festival has been bringing together people from the Ponant Islands, off the western coast, for concerts, discussions, rowing races, cultural events, plays and farmers' markets. The festival highlights the activities of the residents and full-time contributors to the islands' economy, and it's a great success." This is a convincing illustration of solidarity among people who share similar values and lifestyles.

LANGUAGES BY THE HUNDREDS

Given the complexity of their history, it is hardly surprising that islands are home to a vast number of languages. The languages of Oceania are part of the Austronesian group and more than four hundred of them are spoken there, by fewer than three million people. They are subdivided into Melanesian – 350 languages in all, not widely spoken, and including Fijian and Paicî; Polynesian – 40 languages spread from New Zealand to Easter Island and including Samoan, Maori, Tahitian, Futunian and Wallisian; and the 20 Micronesian languages, including Kiribati, Nauruan and Trukic. The Solomon Islands give a good idea of the extent of this astonishing wealth of languages: with its 600,000 people this small archipelago east of Papua New Guinea is home to some eighty native tongues such as Dori'o,

ECONOMIC DEVELOPMENT IS A PRIORITY FOR MANY ISLAND STATES, BUT IT MUST ALLOW FOR PRESERVATION OF THE NATURAL SETTING AND TRADITIONAL CULTURES.

SOME ISLANDS HAVE KNOWN SUCCESSIVE WAVES OF IMMIGRATION FROM AFRICA, EUROPE AND ASIA. EACH HAS LEFT ITS MARK. AND EACH ISLAND IS UNIQUE IN TERMS OF ITS CULTURAL, LINGUISTIC AND RELIGIOUS HERITAGE.

SAFE HAVENS FOR PIRATES, REFUGES FOR SHIPWRECK VICTIMS: THE EXOTICISM OF ISLANDS HAS OFTEN BEEN A SOURCE OF LITERARY INSPIRATION.

Kazukuru, Laghu, Tanema, Vangunu and the charmingly named Guliguli. Some of them, spoken only by a very few individuals, are in the process of becoming extinct, and only three – Kwaio, Are'are and Wara'ae – are spoken by more than 10,000 people. The Solomon Islanders have adopted English as their official language: unsurprisingly, as it is often the language of the colonisers that has helped unify island states. At the same time several official languages can coexist, as in the Seychelles, in the Indian Ocean: French, the language of the first colonisers; Creole, which developed among the African slaves they brought with them; and English, as in 1814 the Seychelles were taken over by the British.
This linguistic variety reflects the astonishing cultural diversity of island peoples, but this heritage is now under threat. Today 96% of the world's languages are spoken by only 3% of its population: in other words, this enormous linguistic wealth is being maintained by a vulnerable minority. It is thought that a language is in danger of disappearing when it has only a very limited number of speakers and is not handed on to the new generation, which is currently the case of about half the Earth's 6,000 languages. It must be remembered that a language is not just a means of communication: words exist also for passing on unique skills, experiences and historical realities. The language of the Inuit peoples of the far north, for example, includes around a hundred words and expressions for different kinds of snow and ice, and when words like these sink into oblivion, entire sections of history and precious human knowledge are lost forever. "When a language disappears every

FISHERMAN FROM THE FRENCH ISLAND OF PORT-CROS, IN THE MEDITERRANEAN.

one of us is dispossessed of its heritage, for then a nation and a culture lose their memory. The same is true of the subtle tapestry that makes our world such a fascinating place." These are the words of Vigdís Finnbogadóttir, former president of Iceland and now a Unesco goodwill ambassador.

Because many island peoples have a strong oral tradition, the disappearance of their languages has an immediate impact on their cultural heritage, whether spiritual or knowledge-based. How are their rites, tales and myths to survive when the words for recounting and transmitting them are no longer understood by anybody? How are ceremonies, celebrations and sacraments to be passed on when the appropriate songs and prayers are translated into a new language? Traditional knowledge, too, is often handed down orally from generation to generation: knowledge of the sea and the weather, the names of plants and animals, recipes, natural medicines, fishing, hunting and farming techniques, and the customs that structure social life. In native island micro-communities these forms of knowledge have played a vital part in maintaining a balance with nature and ensuring sustainable preservation of resources for thousands of years.

Demographic, social, economic and environmental changes, together with the spread of Westernised lifestyles, have had dramatic repercussions for island life. Nonetheless, many of those trying to find ways of guaranteeing sustainable development for island territories are convinced of the value of maintaining traditional knowledge as a source of inspiration for environmental management policies.

SALT-MARSH WORKER IN TULÉAR, MADAGASCAR, IN THE INDIAN OCEAN.

FOLLOWING PAGES: KUNA WOMAN FROM THE SAN BLAS ARCHIPELAGO IN THE CARIBBEAN.
ISLAND DWELLERS FROM WALLIS-AND-FUTUNA, THE FRENCH OVERSEAS TERRITORY IN THE PACIFIC.

CHANGING SOCIETIES

TRADITIONS BASED ON A VITAL LINK WITH NATURE

As natural environments in a state of permanent change, islands have a fragile equilibrium. Their peoples have learnt to be self-sufficient and a deep knowledge of nature handed down from one generation to the next has enabled them to survive for thousands of years in vulnerable settings. Today their specialised knowledge is generating increasing interest from scientists and environmental experts, whose work on biodiversity has led them to realise that many peoples had long ago established systems of soil, forest and fishing management designed to prevent overuse and subsequent deterioration. Traditionally island cultures regulate their land and seafood resources sustainably through sets of rules grounded in long experience. These rules often have a spiritual basis, but they nonetheless evolve in line with environmental change as an ensemble of practices, prohibitions, beliefs and customs that underpin a given society. The solidarity that finds expression in the sharing of wealth, for example, unites and strengthens the community, enabling it to survive even when crops fail or the fish are few. The widespread practice of the taboo aids management of vital natural resources: for instance, hunting and fishing may be forbidden during certain seasons or in certain areas out of respect for the

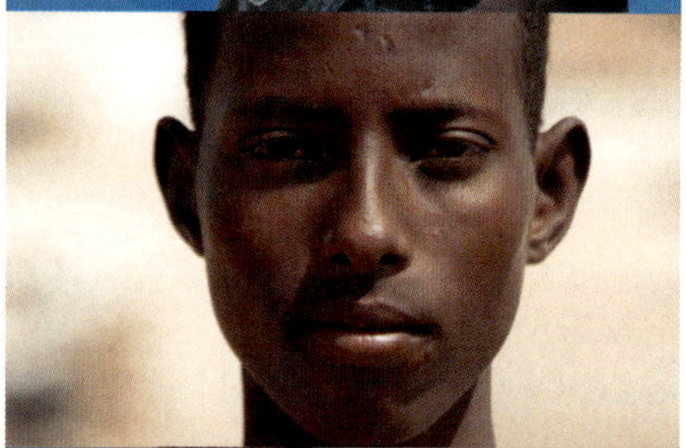

THE DIVERSITY OF THEIR WAYS OF LIFE, CUSTOMS, LANGUAGES AND SKILLS MEANS THAT ISLAND DWELLERS EMBODY AN ENORMOUS – AND ENDANGERED – CULTURAL HERITAGE.

biological cycles of the species concerned. When wood has to be cut, care is taken to preserve the forest canopy so as to protect the soil from erosion by rain. Food gathering is supervised with a view to natural renewal of wild populations. Contemporary resource management and environmental preservation policies are taking increasing account of local exploitation techniques, so often perfectly adapted to native populations' specific environmental, cultural and economic conditions; and many experiments carried out in association with local communities draw on their experience for studies of long-term preservation of resources.

Recognition of local and native skills is a priority for Unesco in its work in the fields of education, science, culture and communication, and the organisation's Small Islands and Indigenous Knowledge section is specifically devoted to the subject. As section head Dr Douglas Nakashima explains, "In many countries local communities have a long history of interaction with the environment. They possess a heritage of knowledge, skills and traditional practices and representations. For native peoples this local knowledge is a key resource in the struggle against marginalisation, poverty and degradation of their living conditions."

The importance of these questions led to the founding of Unesco's LINKS[3] programme in 2002. "Our aim," says Douglas Nakashima, "is to set up synergies between native and scientific knowledge. As Unesco sees it, these synergies between internal and external skills are vital if communities are to make informed choices about their own paths to sustainable development. Thanks to their traditional practices they can survive in a radically changing world while retaining their social, cultural and environmental integrity."

To quote one example, 80% of the world's population continues to treat illness with plants and natural medicines, and over 90% of fishermen still work on an artisanal basis. For this they draw on their detailed, inherited knowledge of the sea to localise and catch the fish and other resources that support their way of life. Their age-old knowledge means they can build their own boats and navigate safely in an unpredictable and sometimes hostile environment. Young people in the pacific are showing real interest in the renaissance of traditional navigation, with its roots in knowledge of currents, sea movement, winds, the stars and marine life. When natural disasters like cyclones and hurricanes occur, Pacific islanders have all the skills needed to rebuild their simple houses. In Fiji the women prepare long-life "hurricane food" which enables survival when the fields have been devastated by storms or flooding. In oral cultures, as Douglas Nakashima points out, "Certain skills are only handed on through action. 'Tradition' and 'heritage' are often taken as synonyms of fixedness, immobility and inflexibility, but in fact local skills are subject to a perpetual process of reassessment, regeneration and extension. Each generation appropriates the cognitive tools and the concepts needed to live in a world of rapid change; and this means adapting ancestral knowledge to your own experience and the possibilities on

P. 46-47: THE LOFOTEN ARCHIPELAGO.

P. 48-49: A HOST OF TRADITIONAL RITES AND CEREMONIES ARE THE CEMENT OF POLYNESIAN SOCIETIES.
TARO PREPARATION AND PIROGUE CONSTRUCTION ON WALLIS-AND-FUTUNA (PAGE 48).
A TRADITIONAL DANCE ON MOORÉA, IN FRENCH POLYNESIA (PAGE 49 AT TOP)
AND TRADITIONAL POLYNESIAN TATTOOS (PAGE 49 AT BOTTOM).

offer. The ease with which native populations adopt modern technology and adapt it to their needs is proof of the inherent dynamism of their knowledge systems."
The Inuit, for example, wasted no time in adopting snow scooters and modern hunting techniques, so despite having become sedentary and living in modern houses, they can still make use of their hunting territories and retain their traditional economy. Modern communication tools also fit well with oral-culture styles of transmission and represent an excellent means of integrating and sharing traditional knowledge and practices.
"For rural and native peoples," Douglas Nakashima concludes, "these traditional systems are the basis for decisions taken locally regarding the fundamentals of daily life, including adaptation to climate change. One of the important, steadily developing aspects of the Unesco LINKS programme is recognition of local and native skills in the monitoring of global environmental change and the measures necessary for adapting to it. Unesco is working with the Intergovernmental Panel on Climate Change (IPCC)[4] with a view to ensuring the same official recognition of traditional knowledge – which includes islander skills – as for scientific expertise.

KASTOM (CUSTOM) IN THE PACIFIC

The islands of Wallis, Futuna and Alofi are situated in mid-Pacific, 2000 kilometres from New Caledonia. In 1959 they decided by referendum to become a French Overseas Territory, while retaining their special status as monarchies within the French Republic.
Three kingdoms coexist in this archipelago of 15,000 inhabitants: Uvea on Wallis, and Alo and Sigave on Futuna. The three kings are named by representatives of the great families – the *aliki* – after the Council of Chiefs has come to an agreement. The kings are assisted by ministers and with them make up a territorial council presided over an administrator who has the rank of Prefect and as such represents the authority of France. Community affairs are governed by customary law. Religion is a major force and its authority is embodied in the Bishop of Wallis and Futuna.
The term *Kastom* covers a number of rites and rules aimed at preserving harmony, peace and the bonds between families and generations. Large-scale traditional ceremonies involving hundreds of people are characterised by exchanges of pigs' tusks, pork, yams and kava, a medicinal root belonging to the pepper family and considered sacred; performances of traditional music and dancing also contribute to communal bonding. *Kastom* is practised on many islands in the Pacific.

A KUNA WOMAN FROM THE SAN BLAS ARCHIPELAGO IN THE CARIBBEAN DISPLAYS THE *MOLA* SHE HAS MADE. OFTEN INSPIRED BY NATURE OR LOCAL LEGENDS, THESE PIECES OF FABRIC ARE PART OF THE TRADITIONAL COSTUME.

Islands in Turmoil

The inhabitants of many small island states are faced with certain hard facts: surrounded by water and in many cases situated in volcanic regions, their territories are especially vulnerable to natural disasters in the form of violent storms, earthquakes and eruptions. Often isolated, they also have to cope with limited resources in terms of fresh water, land and productivity. The result is that their history is studded with calamities that have to be surmounted afresh each time.

IN THE EYE OF THE STORM

THE FURY OF WIND AND WATER

Each year many islands are struck by violent weather episodes which are named differently according to the part of the world in question: hurricanes in the North Atlantic and North-Eastern Pacific, cyclones in the Indian Ocean and typhoons in the North-West Pacific. These phenomena take shape over the ocean in the equatorial zones, beginning with disturbances close to the ocean surface when the temperature of the water reaches or exceeds 26.5°C down to a depth of 60 metres or more. In response to increasing heat and evaporation, hot, moist air rises and is replaced by cooler air at sea level; in turn this cooler air heats up and rises into the atmosphere in the form of spiralling winds which lift water vapour to an altitude of up to 15,000 metres. Then comes the formation of an enormous, revolving cloud that continues to absorb water as wind velocity reaches 350 km/h. The largest of these hurricanes are 1000 kilometres in diameter and attain an average speed of 20–25 km/h. Once the hurricane reaches dry land and loses contact with its water supply, it gradually abates, causing colossal downpours. Especially in the countries the least equipped with storm alert and aid infrastructures, hurricane winds, rain and shock waves regularly cause the deaths of thousands of people, leave hundreds of thousands homeless and wreak havoc to the tune of tens of billions of dollars.
By definition surrounded by water, islands are particularly hard hit by these kinds of events. Every year, for example, the islands of the Caribbean are battered by hurricanes. On average the North Atlantic suffers from eight hurricanes annually – the record so far is 22, in 2005 – and a major destructive event strikes the Caribbean every two years. Each time the result is a human, economic, social and environmental

PREVIOUS DOUBLE PAGE: RABAUL, PAPUA NEW GUINEA: CHILDREN PLAYING IN THE SEA AGAINST THE BACKDROP OF THE ERUPTING VOLCANO TAVURVUR.

disaster and the annual cost to the countries in the region is some 600 million dollars. In a few short hours the benefits of years of development effort can be wiped out. To cite one example: in 1999 Hurricane Lenny devastated the West Indies in a mere two days, with damage in the tiny state of Grenada estimated at 94 million dollars, or 27% of the gross domestic product (GDP). Importantly, Lenny's passage markedly reduced the beach zone, the sand having been carried off by the waves. This kind of erosion has a significant impact on tourism, for while beaches gradually return to their original state, the process takes years. In Grenada coastal protection measures such as planting out the dunes have been taken, with the authorities also doing their best to restrict tourist use of the areas most affected and banning the mining of sand and gravel. However these precautions are futile in the face of the repeated severity of the storms: just five years later, in 2004, Hurricane Ivan struck Grenada and in two hours left behind some 40 dead and flattened 90% of the island's houses. At the same time it devastated the banana plantations, together with the nutmeg fields that provide a quarter of the world's supply. This time overall losses were calculated at more than a billion dollars – twice the GDP for the preceding year. Everything has to be rebuilt before the tourist industry can get back into gear; and nutmeg trees take ten years to reach maturity and full production of their precious crop. Despite aid from the International Monetary Fund, Hurricane Ivan temporarily halted the island's economic development.

KEEPING A WEATHER EYE OUT

The best way of countering these devastating meteorological phenomena is improved forecasting: this means spotting cyclones, hurricanes and typhoons in advance, identifying their trajectory and warning those in their path. This at least means that people can prepare the necessary provisions and take shelter. With this in mind, the World Meteorological Organization (WMO) has set up a programme that includes five Regional Meteorological Centres (RMC) whose specialists track storms as they begin to form over the ocean, study their functioning, assess their force and anticipate their courses. The sooner the alarm is given, the greater the chance of finding adequate protection. The tropical zones have been divided up into five regions, each with a centre to keep a close eye on it. The Cyclones division at the centre in Saint-Denis de la Réunion, for example, monitors the entire south-western part of the Indian Ocean and the information collected is passed on to the authorities, whose responsibility it is to warn the population in the event of a cyclone alert. The action taken depends on the force of the cyclone to come. On Réunion an orange alert signals the arrival of a cyclone in the next twenty-four hours. During that time, it's business as usual, except that nurseries and schools are

closed. A red alert means imminent danger: the population is advised to stay home or find shelter somewhere and remain indoors until further notice.
Prior to these precautions, other basic measures are necessary: houses, for example, must be built to withstand the fiercest winds and must not be too close to the shoreline; and coastal ecosystems such as reefs and mangrove forests must be preserved, since they diminish the force of the waves and thus help limit the impact of the worst storms. Grenada now imposes stricter building standards in relation to distance from the sea and the capacity to resist cyclonic winds and rain.

THE CARIBBEAN: TOGETHER AGAINST THE HURRICANE HAZARD

How do countries whose economy is already fragile cope with compensation and reconstruction when everything has been destroyed? After the devastation caused by Hurricane Ivan, an idea began to germinate: joint insurance coverage for the most vulnerable nations. The result, in 2007, was the Caribbean Catastrophe Risk Insurance Facility (CCRIF), set up by the World Bank and the first intergovernmental risk pooling body in history. The facility's goal is to insure Caribbean states against such natural disasters as hurricanes and earthquakes, and it now provides coverage for 16 island states: Anguilla, Antigua and Barbuda, Barbados, the Bahamas, Belize, the Bermudas, the Cayman Islands, Dominica, Grenada, Haiti, Jamaica, St Lucia, St Kitts and Nevis, St Vincent and the Grenadines, Trinity and Tobago and the Turks and Caicos Islands. In a post-hurricane context the facility provides emergency funding for pressing building needs and for assistance with getting countries back on their feet as quickly as possible. CCRIF also provides member countries with technical assistance in risk assessment, as weather-related natural disasters may well proliferate in a context of climate change. This means calculating average potential losses: Jamaica, for instance, faces a figure of 6% of its GDP, which could increase by 1 to 3 percentage points by 2030.[5] The nations of the Pacific are currently thinking about adopting a similar insurance system, which could also inspire similar protective measures in relation to drought and other disturbances due to climate change.

SHOCKS AND TREMORS

LIVING ON THE RING OF FIRE

Their geological history means islands are more often subject to volcanic eruptions and earthquakes than continental landmasses. Many of them were born along the fault lines separating the oceanic and continental plates: one of these is the Ring

ISLANDS LIVE UNDER THE CONSTANT THREAT OF NATURAL DISASTERS:
HURRICANES AND TORNADOS (TOP LEFT),
VIOLENT STORMS (BOTTOM LEFT)
AND VOLCANIC ERUPTIONS, HERE AT MT STROMBOLI IN ITALY (RIGHT).

HURRICANES CAUSE ENORMOUS LOSS OF LIFE AND DAMAGE, ESPECIALLY THROUGH THE FLOODS THEY BRING.
EVERY YEAR MANY ISLANDS ARE HIT HARD BY NATURAL DISASTERS.

of Fire in the Pacific, an enormous string of islands – home to no less than 452 volcanoes – running along the rim of the planet's biggest ocean. The Aleutians, the Kurils, the Japanese archipelago, the Philippines, the Marianas, the Bismarck Archipelago, the Solomon Islands, Vanuatu, Tonga and New Zealand are all part of this huge, unstable, endlessly shifting geological composite.
Their history is studded with spectacularly lethal disasters. On 26 August 1883, for example, Krakatau, a volcano on the 9 x 5 kilometre Indonesian island of the same name, began to erupt. The next day brought an awe-inspiring explosion, so loud that it was heard several thousand kilometres away. The airborne ash and the tsunami triggered by the tremor caused almost 40,000 deaths on the neighbouring islands and in the region. The island of Krakatau itself all but disappeared. The fate of an entire island, then, can be decided in a matter of hours.

STROMBOLI: THE "LIGHTHOUSE" OF THE MEDITERRANEAN

The volcanic Italian island of Stromboli is part of the Aeolian (or Lipari) Islands. Its area above sea level peaks at 924 metres and the volcano, which descends more than 2,000 metres into the sea, has been in a state of constant eruption for at least 2,000 years. Every twenty minutes or so lava and ash spew from the crater, and more violent explosions are a regular occurrence. The island has been inhabited since ancient times and its inhabitants long made their living from fishing, winegrowing and the cultivation of olives and figs. Down the centuries, though, they have been gradually fleeing, discouraged by the constant eruptions, earthquakes and tidal waves – not to mention the economic difficulties – and most now live off the tourist trade. Nicknamed "the lighthouse of the Mediterranean" because it is visible from a long way off at night, Stromboli is kept under particularly close surveillance by volcanologists.

SURVIVING IN HAITI: NO EASY MATTER

On 12 January 2010 the island of Haiti was shaken by a earthquake measuring 7 on the Richter scale, with tragic consequences: 220,000 dead, 300,000 wounded, the greater part the capital, Port-au-Prince, razed to the ground, and an already fragile economy shattered. How to recover from such a cataclysm? The Haitians had to bury their dead, care for their wounded, rebuild their homes and reorganize

PREDICTION OF WEATHER PHENOMENA IS VITAL FOR PEOPLE LIVING ON ISLANDS:
IT MEANS THEY CAN BE ALERTED IN TIME TO TAKE SHELTER
WITH ADEQUATE SUPPLIES OF FOOD AND WATER.

their public services – notably providing drinking water – while also ensuring the survival of the hundreds of thousands who had lost everything. Following the earthquake the country's economic situation, which had been inching forward over the previous few years, slumped once again, with poverty returning to 2001 levels: 71% of the population living on less than two dollars a day and 50% on less than one dollar – in official terms a state of "extreme poverty".

As part of the process of getting the country back on its feet, the United Nations Environment Program (UNEP) implemented measures for enhancing vulnerable and especially degraded coastal settings and improving their management. The aim was to protect the coastline itself and to ensure the survival of local populations by preserving its resources. Of Haiti's 9 million inhabitants, more than 200,000 live by fishing. This meant that saving the coastal mangrove forest was a priority, as it is among the roots that the larvae and the young of many crustaceans and fish grow and develop. If this natural nursery were to disappear, the entire fishing economy could vanish with it. The mangrove forest also functions as a natural protective barrier, reducing erosion and absorbing 70–90% of the impact of the waves; but many of the trees have been cut down, as their extremely hard wood is used not only as

THE HAITI EARTHQUAKE OF 2010 WORSENED THE PLIGHT OF AN ALREADY POVERTY-STRICKEN POPULATION.
EDUCATIONAL PROGRAMMES ORGANISED BY THE FOPROBIM COMMUNITY ASSOCIATION INCREASE LOCAL PEOPLE'S AWARENESS OF THE NEED TO PROTECT THE NATURAL ENVIRONMENT AS A SOURCE OF FOOD AND OTHER VITAL RESOURCES.

a building material, but also – and mostly – for making charcoal. This in a country whose forest cover has now shrunk to less than 2% of its land surface.
FoProBiM – Foundation for the Protection of Marine Biodiversity – is the sole non-profit Haitian body currently devoted to preserving the marine environment. It was founded by Jean Wiener, a locally born, American-trained marine biologist who has been striving to save his country's ocean for 20 years now. "The 2010 earthquake

mainly hit the cities," he explains, "but the environmental protection programmes were able to continue. This is crucial, as the natural environment provides rural populations with their means of subsistence. It's all the more important in that many city dwellers who lost everything in the disaster have moved to the country to survive, and this puts increased pressure on existing resources." According to the report on the earthquake prepared by the Haitian government, 500,000 people from the major damage areas have taken refuge elsewhere. For the government, "It is vital to systematically include environmental issues in all decisions relating to the process of recovery and development, and to reduce environmental vulnerability, especially through integrated management of watersheds and coastal and marine areas."[6]

HOUSES DESTROYED BY A HURRICANE IN MADAGASCAR. IN JUST A FEW HOURS A NATURAL DISASTER CAN WIPE OUT THE RESULTS OF YEARS OF STRIVING FOR A BETTER LIFE.

FOLLOWING PAGES: EARTHQUAKES AND HURRICANES CAN TRIGGER GIANT WAVES THAT DESTROY EVERYTHING IN THEIR PATH. COASTAL ECOSYSTEMS LIKE CORAL REEFS AND MANGROVE FORESTS CAN ABSORB A SUBSTANTIAL PART OF THE SEA'S IMPACT.

This enabled organisation of the FoProBiM project for mangrove reforestation. Mangrove seedlings are going to be planted in 5-hectare areas on the earthquake-affected sites. They come from a plant nursery which is also a source of substitute species like bamboo, which can be used for making charcoal, and mango, pawpaw, orange, grapefruit and other fruit trees; the point being that the local people will not stop cutting down the mangroves unless they are offered economically viable alternatives: among these is honey-making, which has been especially encouraged among the former mangrove cutters by provision of hives and training in bee-keeping. Another segment of the programme is a plan for cleaning up the shoreline and the degraded mangrove forest: the thousands of plastic containers recovered in this way will be used in the plant nursery.

"The villagers themselves are taking part in the reforestation venture," Jean Wiener continues. "50,000 mangrove trees have already been replanted and the local people keep an eye on the cattle, which are fond of the young shoots. On 8 June 2011 – World Oceans Day[7] – we managed to plant 3,000 mangroves from various nurseries and recover close to 450 kilos of rubbish from a 100-metre section of beach. The quantity of garbage is terrifying."

With UNEP backing FoProBiM is also working on a marine environment awareness and education programme for schools. Teaching aids from Guadeloupe are being adapted to the Haitian context and a teaching kit is going to be given to 500 pupils. Says Jean Wiener, "Our motto is, "Never impose, always propose." As in all developing countries, it's hard for rural Haitians to think in the long term, because they have very few resources and absolutely need this wood. So at the same time as the reforestation programme, we have to take awareness action, especially with children. We try to make them understand the importance of the mangrove

AFTER A HURRICANE THE MALDIVE ISLANDS WERE STRUCK BY TORRENTIAL RAINS (LEFT).
MANGROVE WOOD PRODUCES EXCELLENT CHARCOAL, BUT REMOVAL OF THE FOREST MAKES THE COAST OF HAITI MORE VULNERABLE (RIGHT).

forests for their safety and their future. And because there is an urgent need, we offer the villagers other income possibilities, like honey-making." Several sources of funding, notably the Regional Activity Centre for Specially Protected Areas and Species (SPAW-RAC), housed in Guadeloupe's national park, as well as various private organisations and foundations,[8] have contributed to putting these ventures into action.

APOCALYPTIC WAVES

Another threat hangs over islands: tsunamis, giant waves triggered by an earthquake or a volcanic eruption, but sometimes by an undersea landslip, when one tectonic plate suddenly collides with another. This is what happened on 26 December 2004. The epicentre of the event was northwest of Sumatra, in Indonesia, when a tectonic plate was displaced by 15 metres along some 600 kilometres of the fault line. This slip disturbed the vast mass of ocean water, causing a gigantic tsunami moving at 300–700 km/h. In 2 minutes and 17 seconds it had reached the coast of Sri Lanka, where it killed 35,000 people. Its height when it reached the affected coastlines was 10 to 30 metres, and some hours later it attained East Africa. Indonesia and Sri Lanka were the most affected countries, but many others were very hard hit: in Thailand and India, for example, coastal dwellers were swept away by the ocean's fury. The impact was felt as much as 6,000 kilometres from the epicentre, and dozens of victims were reported on the coasts of Kenya and Somalia. The death toll, in ten countries in all, was 282,000, accompanied by incalculable damage. In Sri Lanka three-quarters of the nation's fishing boats were disabled and most of

VILLAGERS REPLANTING A MANGROVE FOREST IN HAITI.

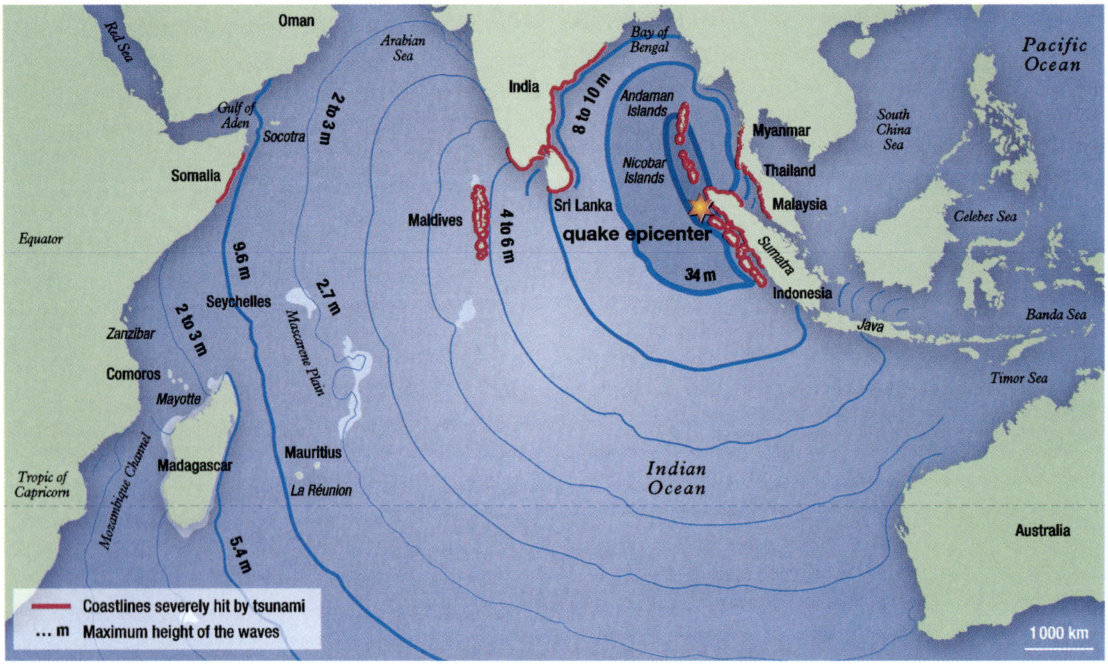

IN 2004 A GIGANTIC TSUNAMI WAS TRIGGERED BY A TECTONIC PLATE SHIFT OFF THE COAST OF SUMATRA.
IN A FEW HOURS THE WAVE HAD MOVED AS FAR AFIELD AS AFRICA,
CAUSING A MASSIVE HUMAN AND ECONOMIC DISASTER.

their owners had no insurance. In the Maldive Islands seawater contaminated more than half the usable land and hundreds of buildings were destroyed. The losses in this Indian Ocean archipelago were reckoned at 66% of GDP. In Thailand the tourist infrastructures on the southwest coast were wiped out. A year later the United Nations came up with an overall damage estimate of 10 billion dollars.

The list of tragedies due to these giant waves is a terrifying one. On 17 July 2006, for example, a tsunami due to an earthquake off the coast of Java killed 668 people. On 29 September 2009 Samoa was hit by a tidal wave that left 190 dead. And then there are the long-term consequences of this kind of event: the passage of the wave leaves fresh water stocks polluted and farmland barren. In Sri Lanka, after the 2004 tsunami, 62,000 wells were contaminated by salt water and water from the sewers. Even large islands are not spared: we all remember the earthquake of force 9 on the Richter scale that struck Japan on 11 March 2011. Its epicentre was at a depth of 24.4 kilometres, more than 100 kilometres from the coast of the archipelago, and the shock was so powerful that the main island of Honshu was displaced by 2.4 metres. It is even said that the earth's axis of rotation shifted by 10 centimetres. This earthquake unleashed a tsunami at least 23 metres high which struck 300 kilometres of coastline, penetrated 10 kilometres inland and devastated an area of at least 500 square kilometres. Aftershocks occurred repeatedly in the days and weeks that followed and the human and economic repercussions were appalling: almost 15,000 dead, 10,000 missing, hundreds of thousands homeless and billions of dollars of damage. The Japanese cataclysm once again highlighted the vulnerability of coastal facilities, especially in the case of nuclear power stations. The near-total destruction of the one in Fukushima had the entire country trembling with fear as a state of nuclear emergency was declared. And together with the people of Japan, the entire world suddenly became aware of the nuclear threats hanging over us all. In the wake of this event and its worldwide impact, Japan announced a plan for saving energy and a turn towards renewable energy calculated to meet 20% of the nation's needs by 2020. The new strategy is based on wind farms built in the sea, geothermal sources and vehicle fuel made from micro-algae. In addition, shoreline management must take greater account of the tsunami threat, as protective walls had proved ineffective against giant waves. But it is also important that outside Japan this tragedy should influence decision-making with regard to development policies in all countries possessing coastlines – and especially island states. Energy facilities built close to the shore must imperatively be made safe, given the marked danger some natural phenomena represent for them.

BECAUSE ISLANDS ARE ESPECIALLY VULNERABLE TO NATURAL DISASTERS,
INTERNATIONAL COOPERATIVE PROGRAMMES HAVE BEEN SET UP
WITH A VIEW TO IMPROVING RESIDENT SAFETY.

TSUNAMIS AND MARINE POLLUTION IN JAPAN

In August 2011, at a press conference on the support being given the Citizen's Radioactivity Monitoring Station (CRMS) in Japan by France's Commission for Independent Research and Information on Radioactivity (CRIIRAD), laboratory director Bruno Chareyon summed up the results of the commission's investigations in Fukushima several months after the accident there: radioactivity rates still 10 to 20 times higher than those regarded as acceptable. Needless to say, the sea itself is polluted, both by windborne radioactive particles and by contaminated water spilling out of the damaged power station. In addition, radioactive particles deposited on land can leach down into rivers and the sea. For the fishermen of the east coast the overall outcome is partial or total discontinuation of their work, depending on the radiation levels detected in fish, official restrictions and customer confidence. Some of the radioactive particles will, of course, be carried across the ocean by currents, while others will settle on the bottom. Specialists consider that radionuclides of the Iodine 131 type, whose half-life is 8 days (i.e., their radioactivity is divided by two every eight days), will remain present for only a few months. On the other hand, caesium 137 and 134, with half-lives of 30 and two years respectively, could continue to pollute the soil and the sea for several years. Terrestrial and marine fauna and flora would then become part of a food chain contamination that could be passed on to people.

Nor does the post-tsunami pollution end there. The 25 million metric tonnes of waste – the metal, plastic, car bodies, houses, and various dangerous products carried out to sea – have sunk and been caught up in the major currents circulating through the northern Pacific, so that their spread will poison marine life further and further afield.

SAFETY IN TIMES OF DISASTER

Unesco's Intergovernmental Oceanographic Commission (IOC), established in 1960 and comprising 138 member-states in 2011, meets the world's need for a body capable of fostering international cooperation and coordinating Ocean research programs, the overall goal being improved management and protection and a lessening of marine hazards (see interview following page). The key words here are, of course, "international" and "cooperation". The Global Ocean Observing System (GOOS) collects physical, chemical and biological data, while the IOC-Unesco works in partnership with other UN bodies and research laboratories to inventory and preserve marine biodiversity, monitor climate change and coordinate tsunami alert systems.

« International cooperation: a weapon against the impact of natural disasters

Interview with Wendy Watson-Wright, IOC-Unesco

WENDY WATSON-WRIGHT IS ASSISTANT DIRECTOR-GENERAL AND EXECUTIVE SECRETARY OF UNESCO'S INTERGOVERNMENTAL OCEANOGRAPHIC COMMISSION. THIS BODY PLAYS AN ESSENTIAL PART IN THE STRUGGLE AGAINST NATURAL DISASTERS BY UNIFYING OCEAN-MONITORING RESOURCES AND BACKING PREVENTION POLICIES.

What do you see as the main threats to the safety of small island developing states (SIDS)?

The biggest problems are rising sea levels and the loss of coastal land and economic infrastructures; acidification of the oceans and subsequent ecosystem upheavals; salinization of coastal water tables; loss of tourist-related infrastructures; and proliferation of major meteorological disturbances.

What mechanisms has the IOC-Unesco come up with to help small island developing states in the event of natural disasters like tsunamis, earthquakes and hurricanes?

With regard to tsunamis, flooding caused by storms, and other events with extreme consequences for coastal areas, the IOC-Unesco advises and assists managers and those in charge of risk reduction policies. It concentrates in the implementation of adaptive measures that reinforce the resilience of vulnerable coastal communities, protect their infrastructures and ensure vital ecological backup. More importantly still, by bringing these small island states together, the IOC-Unesco helps them share experiences, expertise and best practices so as to develop the human and technical resources needed for them to cope with the problems they are facing.

How exactly does the IOC-Unesco's tsunami programme help diminish the consequences of tidal waves?

After forty years' experience coordinating the Pacific Tsunami Warning System (PTWS), the IOC-Unesco is now working on a global alert system as part of a strategy for reducing the effects of natural disasters. Its Tsunami unit is working with member states, other UN agencies and ONGs on setting up a long-term early warning system.

In the wake of the undersea earthquake of 26 December 2004 and the resultant tsunami – one of the worst in history – the IOC-Unesco immediately took charge of coordination, and set about creating the Tsunami Warning System in the Indian Ocean. The latter included advance collection of data from the Pacific Tsunami Warning Centre (PTWC) in Hawaii and the Japanese Meteorological Agency (JMA). This was a temporary measure and on 12 October 2011 it was replaced by three regional surveillance centres in Australia, India and Indonesia, whose mission it is to pass on warnings to national centres.

Living Treasures

The sea forms barriers that separate and isolate islands from the continental land masses. Lost in world's great ocean, island territories are veritable oases – both terrestrial and marine. Sometimes an island is home to forms of animal and plant life that are to be found nowhere else, while, in more general terms, island coastlines, coral reefs, rocky sea-bottoms, marine vegetation habitats and algae coverings teem with life. These environments have been sought out by a host of species seeking to escape predators, find food or reproduce. And the survival of islands' human inhabitants depends on long-term preservation of these natural assets.

LABORATORIES FOR EVOLUTION

DARWIN, THE PRECURSOR

In 1831 a twenty-two year old English naturalist set off aboard the *Beagle* on a world tour that was to last five years. Charles Darwin had been engaged as a naturalist for a scientific expedition, his task being to collect samples and specimens, which he would then identify and classify. On 15 September 1835 the Beagle dropped anchor in the Galapagos Islands, where there were no human inhabitants, and the young naturalist was quick to note that each island was inhabited by different species of birds and turtles. Ultimately his inventory included 13 kinds of chaffinches, 11 wading birds, 25 beetles and 185 flowering plants: "I never dreamed that islands, about 50 or 60 miles apart, and most of them in sight of each other, formed of precisely the same rock, placed under a quite similar climate, rising to a nearly equal height, would have been differently tenanted; but we shall soon see that this is the case."[9] He also noted the singularity of the islands' fauna: "The natural history of these islands is eminently curious, and well deserves attention. Most of the organic productions are aboriginal creations, found nowhere else."[10] After his return to England Darwin published *On the Origin of Species* in 1859 and *The Descent of Man* in 1871. His theory of an evolution of species based on natural selection would shatter the hitherto accepted idea about man's appearance on Earth and revolutionise all the life sciences.

PREVIOUS DOUBLE PAGE: THE WHALE SHARK, THE WORLD'S BIGGEST FISH, CAN BE UP TO 15 METRES LONG.
SPECIMENS REGULARLY COME TO FEED ON ISLAND COASTS IN THE INDIAN OCEAN,
ATTRACTING ADMIRING DIVERS FROM ALL OVER THE WORLD.

MARINE BIODIVERSITY IS A VITAL RESOURCE FOR ISLAND COMMUNITIES,
WHO OFTEN MAKE A LIVING FROM FISHING AND TOURISM:
SEA TURTLES IN THE MOZAMBIQUE CANAL (TOP LEFT),
ANTHIAS IN THE RED SEA (TOP RIGHT), GORGONIAN IN THE MEDITERRANEAN (BOTTOM LEFT),
ANEMONE IN THE RED SEA (BOTTOM RIGHT).

IN MADAGASCAR IT SOMETIMES HAPPENS THAT A WHALE IS TRAPPED IN THE LAGOON:
A WINDFALL FOR THESE VEZO FISHERMEN, WHO CAN FEED THEIR VILLAGE FOR SEVERAL DAYS.

FOLLOWING PAGES: THE SEYCHELLES ARCHIPELAGO IS HOME TO LANDSCAPES UNIQUE IN THE WORLD,
SUCH AS THESE HUGE BLOCKS OF GRANITE ON LA DIGUE, AND THE MAI FOREST
– A UNESCO WORLD HERITAGE SITE – ON PRASLIN.

A NATURALIST'S PARADISE

Since Darwin, islands have been a very special hunting ground for scientists: "It is from here in Madagascar," wrote the French explorer and botanist Philibert Commerson in 1771, "that I can inform naturalists that this is truly their Promised Land. Here nature seems to have withdrawn into a refuge so as to work on models other than those she has used elsewhere: with each step one comes upon the most wonderful, unexpected forms."[11] Since those early times the study of the flora and fauna of the world's islands has made decisive contributions to the natural sciences. It has likewise thrown light on our planet's geological history, climate changes over the aeons, variations in sea level – all of which have influenced the evolution of species – and on the rapid environmental changes caused by human presence: deforestation, pollution, overexploitation of certain species and introduction of non-indigenous plants and animals, to cite only a few examples. On islands, which are small and subject to relatively little interchange with the outside, human activity has a substantial impact, and one that can be more easily measured. Islands are veritable laboratories for living systems.

It has even been the case that scientists have been able to study the occupation of an island in real time. In 1963 an undersea volcanic eruption gave birth to a new island – Surtsey – off the coast of Iceland, which was immediately declared off-limits to humans. Since the very beginning, then, biologists have been monitoring the arrival and development of species, as if they were going back in time and observing the colonisation of a virgin land.

MANY SPECIES ARE TO BE FOUND ONLY ON CERTAIN ISLANDS,
LIKE THIS LEMUR FROM MADAGASCAR (LEFT)
AND THE SEYCHELLES GIANT TORTOISE (RIGHT).

BIODIVERSITY: NO TWO ISLANDS ARE ALIKE

SAFE HAVENS

Characterised by unique sets of flora and fauna that reflect its history and geography, every island represents a distinct ecosystem; and within that ecosystem species have developed to fill specific roles, the overall outcome being an astonishing diversity of evolutionary decisions. To take one example, islands that were once part of a continent are sometimes home to species which have evolved differently from those on the mainland – and even those on other, neighbouring islands. Volcanic and coral islands that have gradually emerged from the ocean build up populations of plants and animals from elsewhere which adapt to their new environment. Then there is the fact that islands often serve as safe havens for birds, animals and plants that no longer exist on the mainland, where they found themselves in unequal competition with other species. This explains the presence of what are called endemic species: life forms found nowhere else. In Madagascar, for example, this is the case for 90% of the plants and 80% of the animals. Islands account for more than half the world's marine biodiversity, as well as for many animal species not to be found on the continents. 13% of Unesco's current World Heritage sites are islands. There is real reason for concern, however, since islands are fragile entities and disturbances to their environments and conditions of life threaten flora and fauna to the point where some species are in danger of being lost forever. Studies have shown that between 66–97% of the endemic plant life in the Galapagos and Canary islands, in the Seychelles, and on Ascension, St Helena, Norfolk Island and Rodrigues, are endangered or actually on the path to extinction.

ISLANDS ARE A GREAT OPPORTUNITY FOR NATURALISTS, AS THEIR LAND AND COASTAL SPECIES HAVE EVOLVED IN ISOLATION: HERE, A CHAMELEON FROM MADAGASCAR (LEFT) AND A TITAN TRIGGERFISH IN THE RED SEA (RIGHT).

BIODIVERSITY IN FRANCE'S OVERSEAS TERRITORIES

With a total of 11 million square kilometres, France has the largest marine area in the world after the United States. It accounts for 10% of the planet's coral reefs and 20% of its atolls, and according to the National Biodiversity Strategy adopted in 2011, its biodiversity is far greater in its overseas territories than in its home waters. With the notable exception of Guyana most of these overseas regions are islands dotted all over the world's oceans: Mayotte, La Réunion and the Eparses Islands in the Indian Ocean; French Polynesia, New Caledonia, Clipperton and Wallis-and-Futuna in the Pacific; the French West Indies in the Caribbean; Saint-Pierre-et-Miquelon in the North Atlantic; and the Australs and Antarctic Islands in the Antarctic Ocean. This provides nature and environment specialists with remarkable scope for study, as no other country in the world has territories in so many latitudes extending from the North Atlantic to the Antarctic.

Inventories of France's overseas possessions bear witness to a truly exceptional biodiversity: 50 times more endemic plants, for example, than in France itself, and in New Caledonia alone a quantity of endemic plant and animal species equivalent to the total for the whole of Europe. On the Eparses Islands – 500 square kilometres of reefs, 44 square kilometres of land – 3 million pairs of birds nest here every year: no less than 40% of the marine birdlife of the Western Indian Ocean. 20% of the species living on the islands are endemic and these waters are home to over 400 species of fish. 22 species of marine mammals are to be found in the vicinity of Mayotte and so far 760 species of fish are listed there.

As in other cases already mentioned, these islands are by nature particularly vulnerable. On La Réunion, for instance, of the original 905 species of local flowering plants and ferns – among them some 100 orchids – 49 are already extinct and 275 are endangered. France has implemented numerous scientific and environmental projects in its overseas territories, with a view to assessing the richness of their ecosystems, understanding how these latter work, predicting changes to come – and taking the necessary protective measures. Man has left his mark, however, in the form of such introduced species as rats, mice, cats and goats, which compete with the indigenous animals and eat the eggs of nesting birds and turtles. Eradication programmes are underway.

«

International protection for networked marine areas

***Interview with Christophe Lefebvre, Marine Protected Areas Agency, France*[12]**

The need for long-term preservation of natural marine assets and sustainable management of overseas territory resources – in a context of necessary socioeconomic development – has led to the creation of Marine Protected Areas (MPAs). These take the form of nature reserves, zones where specific regulations apply or marine nature parks, like those on Mayotte and, since 2012, the Glorieuses (or Glorioso) Islands. The MPAs are crucial to sound ocean governance, but their networking is also important, as Christophe Lefebvre of the Marine Protected Areas Agency emphasises: "Protecting the sea means seeing the ocean in a different light, in terms not of individual issues but of the global context.

To blame the degradation of the sea solely on overfishing is to ignore the complex reality of disruption of marine ecosystems; this is linked to the degradation or disappearance of the habitats provided by mangrove forests, reefs and estuaries, which in the long run can affect people's social, economic and cultural links with the sea. Processing refuse and wastewater before they reach the sea so as to guarantee the quality of seawater is a sign of oceanity. Integrated coastline management is a vital link in the chain of marine ecosystem protection, working from the land towards the sea where the Marine Protected Areas are situated."

If it is to be effective, this integrated management must be worldwide: "The future of the ocean hinges on management of the global marine ecosystem, which means creating and protecting a major network of marine areas. These areas function as observatories for changes in the ocean, refuges for marine fauna, spaces to learn from, sites for renewing fish stocks and zones for ecosystem recovery. They offer invaluable benefits on a considerable scale: ensuring food security; providing sound foundations for blue economies; guaranteeing the well-being of those who use the sea for leisure; preserving and handing on our natural marine heritage; aiding ecological connectivity for the ocean; and making it possible for marine life to adapt to the impact of change. Marine Protected Areas are the underpinning of oceanity. They serve the ocean so that the ocean can serve us. They respond to the needs of the blue economy and the blue society."

SHIFTS IN BIODIVERSITY

A PROGRAMME FOR THE MEDITERRANEAN ISLANDS

The Mediterranean's 10,000 islands and islets are host to a remarkable biodiversity and are often the last refuge of animal and plant species that have disappeared from the nearby continent because of urbanisation, industry and pollution. Working

since 2005 via the Mediterranean Small Islands Initiative (PIM), France's Coastal Protection Agency is putting its mainland and overseas experience to work via operations aimed at protecting and enhancing this shared heritage, while also expanding exchanges of experience and knowledge between the Mediterranean countries. Scientists, nature reserve managers, representatives of official bodies, members of community associations and amateur naturalists are now working together on concrete, grassroots measures for shoreline protection. This project has its roots in the realisation that islands are laboratories on a human scale and as such especially interesting in terms of the study of biodiversity and coastal planning policy.
PIM has come up with a five-pronged approach. The "Terra Cognita" project aims at producing a biodiversity inventory for Big Blue's islands and islets. As Fabrice Bernard, the Coastal Protection Agency's European and international delegate,

SCIENTIFIC STUDY OF THE SMALL ISLANDS OF THE MEDITERRANEAN CLARIFIES THE IMPACT OF HUMAN ACTIVITIES ON BIODIVERSITY AND ENABLES APPROPRIATE MANAGEMENT MEASURES FOR THESE FRAGILE AREAS. HERE, THE ISLAND OF PORT-CROS, OFF THE FRENCH COAST.

explains, "Our scientific expeditions to little known or under-documented sites reproduce the journeys of the 18th-century naturalists. We set off, for example, in the footsteps of Giacomo Doria, an Italian nobleman who travelled the Mediterranean aboard the *Volante* in 1875–78, discovering and describing the terrestrial and marine flora and fauna of the Italian, Greek and Turkish islands. Since 2005 PIM has inventoried 80 islands and islets. We're updating what's already been done and at the same time identifying species in areas that had never been looked at."

Two other projects, "Pharos" and "L'Atelier des îles" (The Islands Workshop) have to do with sharing of knowledge and experiences (see page 234), while "Albatros" monitors marine birdlife. Last but not least, the "Iles Sentinelles" (Sentry Islands) programme tracks the impact of global changes on the biodiversity of the Mediterranean islands. For the specialists involved there are all sorts of advantages in this choice: the area is small and there are fewer different environments: this means fewer species and simpler food chains. Scientific observation is easier and because processing of results is rapid, appropriate management solutions can be organised relatively quickly. These operations also lend themselves to regular and long-term regional checking of the impact of environmental changes.
"The big challenge now," continues Fabrice Bernard, "is to quantify marine and terrestrial biodiversity, to equip these islands with measuring devices for temperatures,

IN A NUMBER OF MEDITERRANEAN AREAS RESTRICTIONS ON POLLUTION AND OVERFISHING HAVE BROUGHT REVIVAL AND REPLENISHING OF DEGRADED SEA BOTTOMS.

pollution, etc., and to monitor the situation over the decades to come. That way we will really be able to measure the impact of global changes – not just climate change. We want to set up a network of around twenty islands covering the whole Mediterranean rim and use it to point the way for future generations." Islands like Riou, off Marseille, Filfal to the southwest of Malta and the Galita archipelago in Tunisia are going to be used as "sentries". For the moment most of the islands chosen are in the western Mediterranean basin, but eventually the programme will embrace all the Big Blue countries.

The Sentry Islands project focuses especially on the consequences of the arrival of "invasive" species, biological invasions being one of the main causes worldwide of the disappearance of species and the decline of biodiversity. On many Mediterranean islands certain exotics like the sea fig (*Carpobrotus edulis*) colonise very fast, to the detriment of local species. In addition animals like the rat, which comes ashore from ships, multiply and upset the life cycle of the fauna, in particular by eating the eggs of birds and turtles. Because these islands are small the impact of human activity is felt very quickly, but interestingly, this also means that conservation measures can bring rapid turnarounds: in several cases, for example, rat eradication programmes have enabled recreation of bird populations in just a few months.

ORIGINALLY FROM THE PACIFIC, THE LIONFISH IS NOW MULTIPLYING IN THE CARIBBEAN, WHERE IT COMPETES WITH LOCAL SPECIES.

SEA INVADERS

Marine biodiversity also suffers from the arrival of species from elsewhere, as these can compete with local species, sometimes to the point of taking their place. Invasive species are among the main threats to biodiversity in the Mediterranean: biologists counted 916 of them in 2008, as against 814 in 2007 and 571 in 2005.[13] This corresponds to the introduction of a new alien species every ten days. Most of these species enter "naturally" via the Suez Canal (51%) or the Straits of Gibraltar (7%).[14] Other vectors are ships' water ballast (28%), aquaculture (8%) and various other activities such the trade in living marine organisms (6%). Thus significant changes are being observed in the Mediterranean, but it is hard to know if the newly identified species were already present or if they have only just arrived. This uncertainty can only be resolved by regular monitoring and ongoing inventories.

Similarly, in 1985 the waters of the Caribbean revealed the presence of the venomous *Pterois*, or Lionfish, a native of the Indo-Pacific which began to reproduce significantly in 1992. Several of these fish probably escaped into the sea when an aquarium in southern Florida was damaged by a hurricane. This predator proliferated along the southeast coast of the United States, then moved into the waters of the Bermudas and the Bahamas; they are now well established and sightings have been reported as far away as Cuba, Puerto Rico and down the South American coast. Reaching maturity in about twelve months, the *Pterois* reproduces all year

THE LAGOON AROUND MAURITIUS IS HOME TO A ENORMOUS VARIETY OF FISH AND MARINE INVERTEBRATES WHICH COME TO BREED IN THIS SHELTERED SETTING.

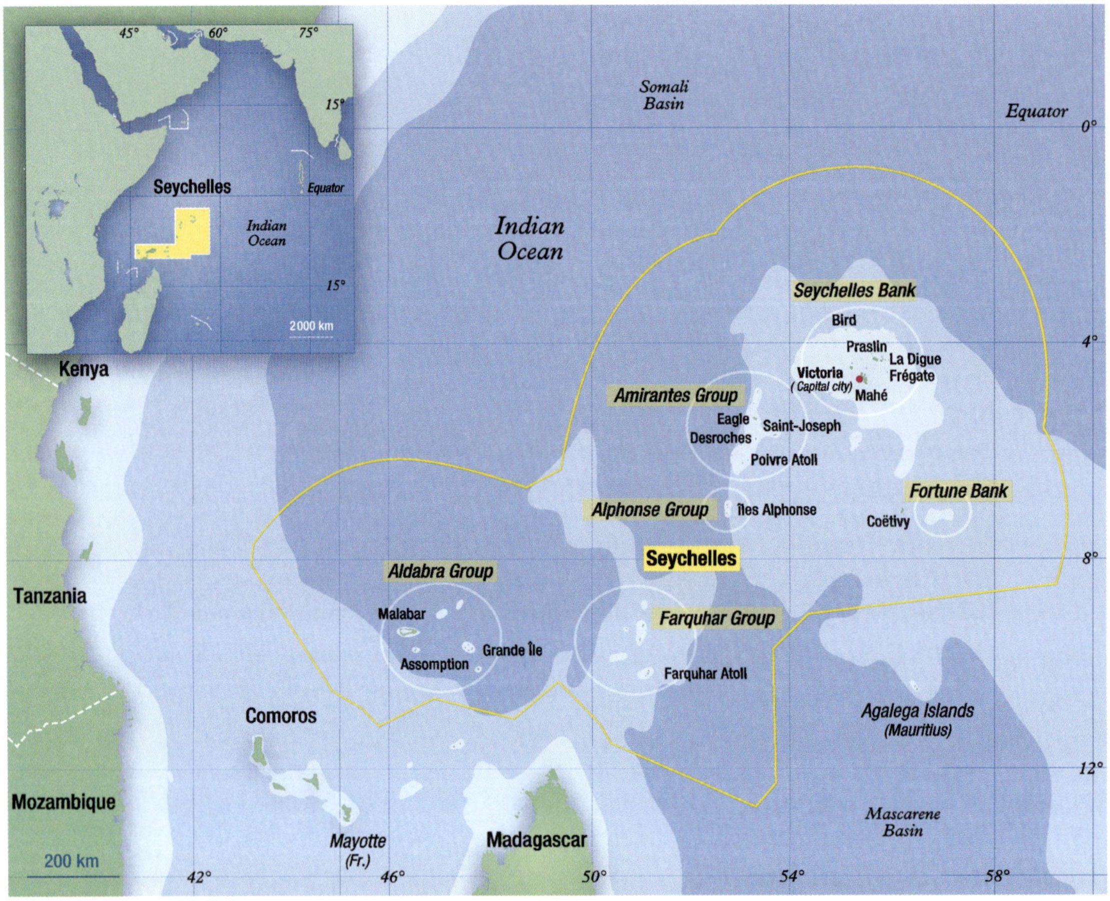

THE SEYCHELLES ARCHIPELAGO IN THE INDIAN OCEAN COMPRISES 115 ISLANDS SPREAD OVER AN IMMENSE MARINE TERRITORY. THE LAND AREA IS ONLY 455 SQUARE KILOMETRES, BUT THE NATION'S EXCLUSIVE ECONOMIC ZONE IS 1,336,559 SQUARE KILOMETRES!

round, laying 30,000 eggs at each spawning period. Apart from certain big groupers and trevally, it has no natural predators in its new environment. Covered with venomous spines, this voracious, aggressive species competes with the native Caribbean fish and drives them out of its hunting territories. In this way the *Pterois* disrupts food chains and the general balance of the reef. A single large individual can consume as many as twenty small fish in half an hour.

The potential economic consequences for local fishing and tourism are cause for real concern. In the Bahamas a national action plan has been launched by the Ministry of Fishing and the Marine and Environmental Studies Institute (MESI). REEF, a network of professional divers, has likewise set up a programme to combat the invader in the Caymans, the Bahamas, the Turks and Caicos Islands and the Dutch West Indies. The divers are specially trained to identify the poisonous *Pterois*, capture them and take action in case of stings. So far the several hundred captured by divers have been integrated into a database that allows for monitoring of this biological invasion.

In Guadeloupe, Franck Mazéas works for the Department of the Environment, Development and Housing (DEAL) and the French Coral Reef Initiative (IFRECOR). He supervises the inventorying of the *Pterois* and is sufficiently concerned about the effects of its proliferation to have set up a programme to counter the invader: "Over the last two years this fish has been multiplying at a dramatic rate, and now the whole of the West Indies is concerned, including Martinique and Guadeloupe. This isn't the first case of species invasion in Guadeloupe, but it's a very special one: the *Pterois* is a danger to local marine fauna, but most of all it's extremely venomous; if it feels threatened by a diver, for instance, it can sting him and the shock creates a state of respiratory distress. What's more, the *Pterois* is easily caught in nets and traps; and while the fisherman of the Indo-Pacific are long since acquainted with the dangers it represents, this isn't the case in the Caribbean and the risk of accidents is high." This is why professionals have to be alerted, specialist capture teams set up and people encouraged to eat the *Pterois*, whose flesh is much appreciated by gourmets. At the same time toxicity tests are currently under way, as certain reef fish – including the *Pterois* – are sometimes contaminated by microalgae that cause serious food poisoning. If the test results are favourable, encouraging consumption of the *Pterois* would help limit its numbers. There is even talk of issuing recipes accompanied by advice on removing the fish's venom sac. In another, ingenious project the managers of the marine park on Roatan, a small island in the Honduras, had the idea of feeding dead *Pterois* to sharks: the latter seem to have no problem with the venomous sting, and have now taken the stratagem one step further by adding live *Pterois* to their hunting menu.

TOP: THE COCO DE MER *(LODOICEA MALDIVICA)* GROWS ONLY IN THE SEYCHELLES. MUCH SOUGHT AFTER BY COLLECTORS, ITS DISTINCTIVE BUTTOCKS-SHAPED NUT IS NOW PROTECTED AND TRADE IS STRICTLY REGULATED.

BOTTOM: LOCAL FRUIT, VEGETABLES AND OTHER FARM PRODUCTS ARE THE BASIS OF ISLAND FOOD CONSUMPTION, BUT ARE UNDER THREAT – LIKE THEIR PRODUCERS' INCOME – FROM IMPORTS.

THE WEB OF LIFE

PRESERVING ENVIRONMENTS AND SPECIES

For the Seychelles archipelago preservation of biodiversity is vital to the survival of the country's two main economic activities: fishing and tourism. "Biodiversity is acutely sensitive to environmental change," explains specialist Lindsay Chong Seng, former director of the Seychelles Island Foundation, which manages Aldabra Atoll and the Mai Valley Nature Reserve on the island of Praslin, both on the Unesco World Heritage List. "Island species have evolved in isolation and they're not equipped to compete with more aggressive species. In a way you could call them living dinosaurs."

This is exactly what the visitor feels on Aldabra, a thousand kilometres southwest of the main Seychelles island of Mahé. Made up of reefal limestone, the atoll covers 155 square kilometres and encloses a vast lagoon. For at least 200,000 years it has been home to *Geochelone gigantea*, the Aldabra giant tortoise, whose males weigh up to 300 kilograms. Currently there are over 100,000 of them, which makes this the biggest tortoise colony in the world. The atoll has doubtless been protected by its isolation: it has no landing strip and getting there by boat from Mahé takes four days. Moreover, there are no streams or rivers, no soil for agriculture and no guano. "That's no doubt why the environment has remained intact," explains Lindsay Chong Seng. "The Seychelles are lucky in having two listed sites: we finance the research and protection programs on Aldabra with the admission fee paid by tourists visiting the Mai Valley, which is much more accessible and only an hour by boat from Mahé." Mai Valley, on the small island of Praslin, is a true natural treasure: it offers primeval forest rich in endemic plants and animals and is home to *Lodoicea maldivica* – the Coco de Mer – found nowhere else in the world. Its famously buttocks-shaped fruit, whose nicknames include Sea Coconut and Love Nut, can weigh up to 20 kilograms; its shape, however, nearly brought about its extinction, for the nuts are much sought-after by collectors. However, the trees are now legally protected and trade in the nuts is strictly regulated.

BIODIVERSITY: VITAL FOR PEOPLE TOO

For many years the inhabitants of the Seychelles gave little thought to homeland biodiversity. The tall trees were cut down by the first settlers for ships and houses, the eggs of marine birds were collected en masse and thousands of tortoises and turtles were slaughtered. But as Lindsay Chong Seng points out, change over the last few years has been positive, with a new awareness of the value of the marine and terrestrial environments: "Turtle cartilage was dried and shipped in tons to London for making turtle soup. Then we gradually realised that this wasn't a sustainable state of affairs: we began by banning the taking of the biggest turtles; then only males; and finally, twelve years ago, a blanket ban was imposed. We even got funding from the World Bank to retrain people who had been living off the turtle industry. Since then there's been a spectacular increase in numbers. And overall, I feel that the growth of tourism is a good thing: in the old days all the virgin forest was being cut down to make way for coconut palms and cinnamon, to the detriment of many indigenous species. Since the 1980s the approach has been more ecotouristic, with visitors coming to enjoy the advantages of the natural setting: diving, birdwatching, botanising, etc. Things have really changed and even the local young people are bent on finding the best ways of managing our natural assets. Needless to say, our marine resources must also be used properly: the Indian Ocean Tuna Commission (IOTC) is doing a great job of monitoring fishing, and our shallow-water areas are restricted to subsistence fishing only. Destructive techniques like fishing with cyanide and dynamite never became widespread here. It has to be said, too, that we have a small population living on a vast marine territory of 115 islands."

The Seychelles also have their own biodiversity community association in the form of the Marine Conservation Society. One of its founders and spokesmen is Dr David Rowat, born in the UK but a resident for twenty-six years and now a naturalised Seychellois: "We work in several fields. In conjunction with the hotels we have set up conservation programmes for marine turtles on the nearby beaches and we check the populations regularly. We're also working on whale sharks."

The world's biggest fish – up to 15 metres long – the whale shark migrates from August to October up the coast of Madagascar and the Comoros and then to the Seychelles where it stays on, feeding close to the surface. "It's a perfect opportunity for observation," David Rowat continues. "We began studying them in 1996, financing the programme with the income from the tourists who come to admire them."

Constructible land is in short supply in the Seychelles, and local elected representatives are constantly in search of sites for housing, industry and tourist infrastructures. There are even artificial islands like Eden Island, made from reclaimed coral rubble and used for building luxury homes for sale mainly to foreigners. David Rowat has noticed that the impact of this urban and industrial development is often misunderstood or feared by political leaders and the general public: "Our third line of action is development along the coastline. We are currently using two pilot sites to establish methods that will limit the effects of human activity on vulnerable areas, and at the same time working on environment awareness and education. Environmental impact studies are often heavy going and hard to understand, so we've come up with educational material explaining, for example, the building of a hotel or a desalination plant, so that everyone can understand the changes they're going to bring and the possibilities for influencing the decision-making process." Working this way often leads to long-term measures for avoiding damage that would have serious environmental, economic and social consequences.

BIODIVERSITY: THE KEY TO RESILIENCE

The relationships between living species intermesh to form the "web of life" in which each thread has its part to play. Diversity – of environments, species and genes – is vital to the sound functioning of our planet, for it enables us to get the best out of the combined resources of a given context. The more species there are practising different ways of living, the more resilient the ecosystem is: the more capable it is of a return to normal in the wake of disruption. But while a strong, healthy, diversified ecosystem can recover after radical change, it cannot do so indefinitely. In a context of repeated onslaughts – from pollution for example – its resilience will lose its edge, just as in the case of someone who is recurrently ill: gradually the victim weakens and loses his immune defences, until one day he is unable to resist an attack by some new microbe. Each time the return to a state of good health is longer and more difficult.

Biodiversity is essential to the ecological balance not only of islands, but also of the entire planet. As Lindsay Chong Seng so neatly puts it, "It's like the canaries miners used to take down the pit: when the air was too vitiated, the bird died and the miners knew they had to get back to the surface fast. For me these islands are our planet's canaries. There's another image, too: if our world was spaceship *Earth* and the species were its components, it could still fly minus a few of them – one or two nuts and bolts aren't necessarily critical – but its overall structure would be weakened with each loss. And if a missing part is vital to the functioning of the whole, or if too many parts are damaged or missing, a wreck is inevitable. You never know which component, if it suddenly goes missing, is going to trigger disaster."

A CHANGE OF HEART

With its 750 square kilometres Dominica, in the Caribbean, remains an authentic natural paradise overlooked by mountains topped with primeval forest. Many species of cetaceans come to spend the winter in its warm coastal waters and this is one of the world's great spots for observing the sperm whales that live here all year round. November to March is especially rewarding: this is when the females give birth. Dominica is home to the last descendants of the Caribbean Indians and whaling was long practised in the traditional manner here. For a number of years the local fishing industry, as in other countries in the region, received financial support from Japan; and in return Dominica backed the Japanese during votes on commercial whale hunting at the International Whaling Commission sessions. This stance caused widespread protest, in particular from the French West Indies – Martinique and Guadeloupe – which were in the process of creating a refuge for marine mammals. Moreover, it badly tarnished the nation's image within the tourist industry. Ultimately the government decided to make an about-turn: it announced in 2008 that it would not vote for whaling and confirmed this position in 2011. However other island states in the Caribbean – Antigua and Barbados, St Kitts and Nevis, Grenada, St Lucia, and St Vincent and the Grenadines – continue to support the countries that still practise whaling.

PREVIOUS DOUBLE PAGE: OF THE EIGHT SPECIES OF BAOBAB IN THE WORLD, SEVEN ARE TO BE FOUND IN MADAGASCAR AND SIX OF THOSE ARE ENDEMIC – THEY EXIST NOWHERE ELSE IN THE WORLD. THE STRANGE MARKS ON THE TRUNK SEEM TO BE DUE TO A DISEASE.

SPERM WHALES CAN BE UP TO TWENTY METRES LONG. THEY OFTEN LIVE IN GROUPS, WITH THE FEMALES ACCOMPANIED BY THEIR YOUNG. HUMAN BEINGS CAN APPROACH PROVIDED THEY ARE CAREFUL NOT TO DISTURB THEM.

Small Island States

In a globalised world constantly shaken by ecological, energy and economic crises, islands play a distinct, if often discreet part. The media remain focused on the giants of our planet – China, the United States and Europe – but a look at the way things are evolving in small island states could teach the rest of the world a great deal about current windows of opportunity for human settlements and about development choices conducive to a more stable future.

A "SPECIAL GROUP" OF COUNTRIES AND TERRITORIES

SMALL ISLANDS: ALMOST A QUARTER OF THE WORLD'S NATIONS

Drawing up a list of small island states is no easy matter: obviously geographical criteria such as land area are crucial, but a wide range of political and socioeconomic factors also has to be taken into account. At the Earth Summit in Rio in 1992, a "special group" was pinpointed within the United Nations' 192 members: Small Island Developing States (SIDS). Numbering some fifty in all – close to a quarter of the world's nations – the group is represented in all the planet's seas: the Pacific, Atlantic and Indian Oceans, the Caribbean, the South China Sea and, for Malta and Cyprus, the Mediterranean. It also includes a handful of low-altitude coastal states – Guinea-Bissau, Belize, Surinam – and non-independent entities such as French Polynesia. Strictly speaking this is not a grouping of states, but its goal is to bring together territories sharing various characteristics and problems and interested in forming a network. The overall purpose is to set development objectives that will enable them to deal more effectively with specific issues. Each member of the group has its particular form of geographic vulnerability to cope with, which means that all of them need to build their capacity to face the economic and environmental challenges of today's world.

In the interests of greater international visibility 43 of them have formed the Alliance of Small Island States (AOSIS), comprising 39 United Nations member states, and four non-member "observers": American Samoa, Guam, the Netherlands Antilles, and the U.S. Virgin Islands (see map, page 18).

PREVIOUS DOUBLE PAGE: THE ISLAND OF MALÉ, CAPITAL OF THE MALDIVES, HAS 104,000 INHABITANTS ON A MERE 5.8 SQUARE KILOMETRES OF LAND. AN ARTIFICIAL ISLAND HAS BEEN CREATED TO REDUCE OVERCROWDING.

PHILIPS

ARCHIPELAGO LIVING

Many island states are in fact archipelagos composed of up to a hundred islands; in other words they have a small, fragmented land area spread over a vast marine territory. The Kiribati Islands, for instance, are home to a little over 100,000 people and are made up of three south-western Pacific Ocean archipelagos situated thousands of kilometres from each other. The Gilbert Islands – 17 atolls, including Tarawa, site of the capital, Bairiki – are 1,500 kilometres from Fiji. 1,800 kilometres east of the Gilberts are the eight atolls of the Phoenix Islands, and further away still are the Line Islands, whose 11 atolls are 3,300 kilometres from the capital. Not to be forgotten, either, is the isolated island of Banaba, west of the Gilberts and the only non-atoll in the entire group. For Kiribati, maintaining connections between its scattered atolls is an extremely costly headache: to get from Tarawa to the Line Islands, for example, you have to go via Fiji, Hawaii or the Marshall Islands, the kind of situation that poses real problems for tourism, with its insistence on speed and cheapness, and for the various local economies as a whole. Getting to neighbouring islands and continental regions is likewise a very expensive business.

In this kind of archipelago everything – water, energy, consumer goods – has to be transported from one island to the other. In most cases public institutions are on the main island – where the capital is – but infrastructures are fragmented and the people living in the most distant territories often have limited access to schools, hospitals and government offices. Costs are high and the quality of the services provided sometimes suffers – a state of affairs economists refer to as "double insularity".

Island economies have no choice but to adapt to this singular situation: transport costs weigh heavily in the balance for both imports and exports, and the further the island is from its nearest continent, the higher these costs are. In addition, islands provide only a limited market, which means less competition and still higher prices for imported goods. Tourism, of course, depends on available means of air and sea transport, and this raises such issues as cost, organisation, frequency and the effects of bad weather. At the same time, however, distance and isolation are used by travel operators to heighten the appeal of destinations like these. The overall result, then, is a host of local details that have to be taken into consideration in the context of development programmes.

SHARED CHARACTERISTICS

An immense marine area and a meagre, often fragmented quantity of land surrounded by water: these are the basic givens for any understanding of the constraints islands are subject to. Their vulnerability, however, does not hinge solely on these

TRAVEL BETWEEN THE ISLANDS OF AN ARCHIPELAGO IS BY BOAT OR PLANE.
THE ECONOMY DEPENDS TOTALLY ON THE FACILITIES FOR TRANSPORTING PASSENGERS AND GOODS.

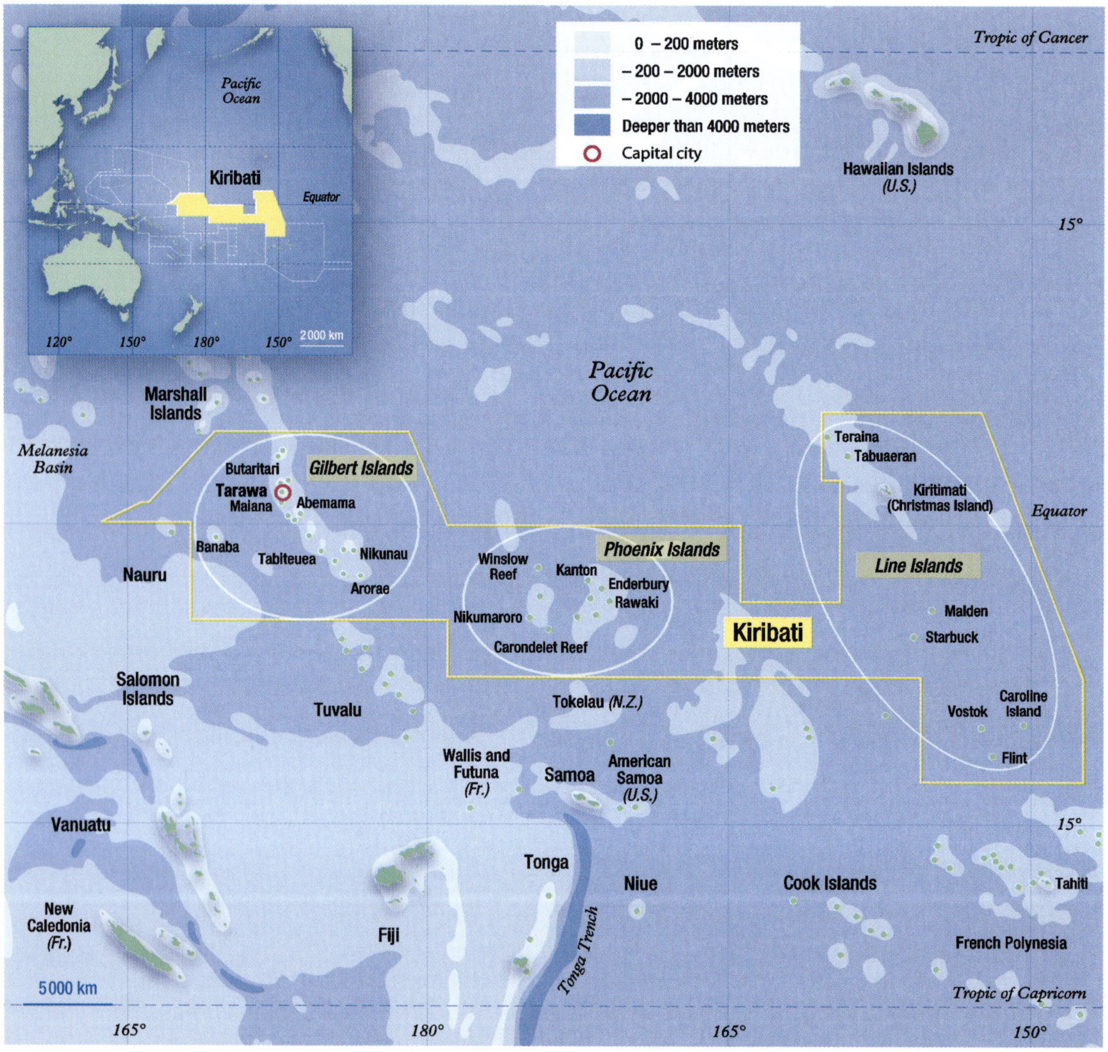

THE SIZE OF SOME ARCHIPELAGOS TAXES THE IMAGINATION. SPREAD ALONG THE EQUATOR IN THE PACIFIC, THE REPUBLIC OF KIRIBATI HAS A GIGANTIC AREA, WITH MORE THAN 3,000 KILOMETRES BETWEEN THE CAPITAL, TARAWA, AND THE OUTLYING LINE ISLANDS.

geographic characteristics and the impact of natural and environmental disasters. While often very different in terms of location, size and history, islands have a number of shared characteristics due to demographic and economic contexts that make them more vulnerable in terms of coping with the fortuities of the global economy.

Most islands have only limited resources and the lack of economic diversification makes them fragile: the local economy is dependent on one or two principal sectors, the others being insufficiently developed to ensure a presence on the international market. As a rule industry plays a very minor role in a context dominated by farming and services. In addition, significant rises in tourism and the adoption of modern lifestyles and consumption practices mean even more pressure on the land and local resources.

Fortunately, small island developing states have all sorts of assets: marine wealth, strategic positions, natural heritage and capacities for adaptation and resilience that are real strengths in a world of rapid change.

BUILDING ECONOMIC AUTONOMY

SMALL, OVER-POPULATED TERRITORIES

Population concentration on islands can sometimes reach alarming proportions: even Manhattan, with more than 25,000 residents per square kilometre, can seem deserted by comparison. The most densely populated island in the world is tiny Santa Cruz del Islote, part of Colombia, whose 0.01 km^2 is home to 1,240 people – a staggering density of 125,000 people per km^2. Its schools, football pitches and cemeteries are on neighbouring territories and all water is brought in by boat. Hong Kong's Ap Lei Chau island succeeds in fitting no fewer than 87,000 people into an area of 1.32 km^2 plated with skyscrapers. Demographic explosion had brought Malé, the main island of the Republic of Maldives to a total of 104,000 by 2011, one result being the creation of two artificial islands several kilometres to the north: Hulhulé for the airport and Hulhumalé, made of sand, for the capital's population overspill.

Ebeye, part of the Marshall Islands, has been nicknamed "the shantytown of the Pacific". Its 15,000-plus people on an area of 0.35 km^2 add up to a density of around 42,000 per km^2. Many of the inhabitants – half the population is under 18 – work in the big American base on a neighbouring island. Sanitation on Ebeye leaves much to be desired and health problems are rife. Other, historical factors continue to impact the life of Marshall Islanders: at the end of World War II the islands became a United States trust territory, and until the late 1960s the Americans used Bikini Atoll, part of the group, for a total of 67 atmospheric nuclear tests. The first H-bomb trials were carried out there in 1952, and Castle Bravo, the most

ISLAND STATE ECONOMIES OFTEN DEPEND ON A SMALL NUMBER OF SECTORS:
CULTIVATION OF COCONUT PALMS FOR COPRA (TOP) OR INDUSTRIAL-SCALE FISHING (BOTTOM),
WITH FISHING LICENCES BEING SOLD TO FOREIGN COMPANIES.

FOLLOWING DOUBLE PAGE: ISLANDS ARE NOT CUT OFF FROM THE REST OF THE WORLD
AND DEPEND LARGELY ON OTHER COUNTRIES FOR BASIC SUPPLIES.
SOMETIMES THEIR OIL COMES FROM A LONG WAY AWAY, WHICH MAKES ENERGY EXPENSIVE.

powerful American test ever, literally shook the atoll in 1954. Repeated exposure to radiation has left the local population with abnormally high rates of cancer and those who fall ill are obliged to seek medical care elsewhere.
How is a steadily growing number of men, women and children to be provided with food and water when local resources are strictly limited? How are refuse and wastewater to be disposed of, infrastructures developed and adequate development ensured for an endlessly expanding population? These problems are especially acute in the island context, but not limited to it: today the entire planet is facing the same critical challenges.

MARKED DEPENDENCE ON THE CONTINENTS

Links with major continental countries are especially important for island states, and this explains the strange event that took place recently in Samoa, situated on the 180th meridian in the Pacific Ocean: 30 December 2011 vanished from the calendar. The Samoans saw the sun go down on Thursday 29th and rise again, a few hours later, on Saturday 31st. The government had simply decided to change time zones by displacing the international dateline a little to the west, making Samoa one of the first countries to see the dawning of the new day. The reasons for the decision were economic, as prime minister Tuilaepa Sailele Malielegaoi explained: "We lose two working days every week: When it's Friday here, it's Saturday in New Zealand; and when we're at church on Sunday the working week is already underway in Sydney and Brisbane." The United States, to the northeast, were long Samoa's main trading partners, but have now been replaced by Australia and New Zealand, to the west; and the time difference, formerly some twenty hours, is now only one and three hours for Wellington and Sydney respectively. The island of Tokelau, a New Zealand dependency, has made the same choice. By contrast, American Samoa remains east of the dateline and has a 23-hour time difference with Apia – the Samoan capital – which is only a hundred kilometres and 40 minutes by plane away. All maps of the world are going to be changed to accommodate a dateline modification which illustrates perfectly how crucial continental connections are for island states.
Islands depend on continents for a significant part of their materials, energy and consumer goods: because they are small they have only limited resources in terms of farmland, forests and minerals, and building space for houses, factories and public infrastructures; this situation has been exacerbated by population growth and the shift from a subsistence to a globalised economy. On any island most merchandise comes from outside, by boat or even by plane, and so costs much more than on the continent. At the same time, though, small island states have to meet the needs of their people: they finance imports by exporting local commodities – sugar, fruit,

fish and other marine products, pearls, spices, coffee, essential oils, textiles, etc. – but their markets are far away and as a rule their exports lack diversity. When an island has a "flagship product" – nutmeg in Grenada, for example – it has a niche that ensures its place in the world economy. But unforeseen change can have critical side-effects, especially in small, independent island states: rocketing oil prices push up production and transport costs, and put a brake on exports, as has been the case with shrimp in Madagascar. A hurricane can destroy harvests, a political crisis or a conflict can scare tourists away, and pollution can poison fish and seafood, with massive repercussions for the local economy.

What remains essential for islands' survival, then, is their capacity to regenerate and to adapt both to social and environmental upheavals and to the changing nature of the international market.

THE LOFOTEN ISLANDS: LIVING BY FISHING

Islands belonging to a continental country – the Lofotens, for example, which are part of Norway – are also faced with the problem of economic independence. Situated in the Norwegian Sea, within the Arctic Circle, these mountainous, wildly beautiful Viking islands enjoy a relatively mild climate thanks to the warmth of the Gulf Stream; however the combination of steep coastlines and strong winds make farming all but impossible. The residents export a little meat and milk, but all other consumer goods have to be imported from the mainland, with the islanders depending on the sea for most of their income. Whaling is a traditional activity in these cold waters; the Norwegians continue to hunt several hundred rorquals and minke whales each year and as it happens, the country's main whale processing centre is on the island of Skrova, in the north-eastern Lofotens. Today virtually all of the islands' 24,000 inhabitants live off fishing: in addition to the cod that make up the bulk of the catch, they also net herring, halibut, haddock, hake and squid. Known locally as *skrei*, the cod come from the Barents Sea during February–April to spawn in the waters around the Lofotens, and once caught they are either frozen or sun-dried on racks – a centuries-old tradition. Much of the output is exported to European countries, especially Italy, where salt cod is considered a real delicacy. Because of overfishing, however, in the early 1980s stocks of cod plummeted; the fishing industry went into crisis and unemployment hit many families. In 1989 a system of quotas was introduced, together with limits on the fishing season and the introduction of cod-farming. Today, improved management of marine resources has led to a rise in fish populations and a revival of the local fishing industry, but the people of the Lofotens have realised how dangerous it can be to put all your (fragile) eggs in one basket, and they are now looking to diversify their sources of income. Offshore oil drilling projects have been talked about, but pollution due to oil spills represents a permanent danger to both fishing and tourism; the result being that environmentalists have called for Unesco World Heritage listing for the islands, which would also provide an additional attraction for the region.

VITAL ASSETS: RESILIENCE AND ADAPTABILITY

As long as demographic growth and pressure from human activity on the natural setting were not excessive, the needs of island dwellers were met by their land and marine resources. However, environmental change, notably in such forms as the intensive farming of bananas and sugar cane that developed during the colonial era, together with the move towards a globalised economy, have shifted the balance. To take just one example, local products like eggs, chicken and pigs cannot always compete pricewise with imports from Asia and South America. So in order to become more competitive and ensure food autonomy, island-based producers must modernise.

A further factor is that island dwellers – whose overall numbers are rising rapidly – have legitimate aspirations to a higher standard of living. New demands are being heard, and this means that island states need to develop resource-based economic sectors – their natural setting, their specific farm products, their marine territory – that will finance the necessary imports. Small islands can also count on other assets for ensuring economic and social growth: flexibility and the capacity to react quickly to change. Island settings are quicker to feel the effects of economic and environmental upheavals, but the other side of the coin is that implementation of development programmes is faster and less complicated. On smaller territories, where business activity is restricted and populations less numerous, it is easier to come up with positive initiatives and economic alternatives. On the other hand, local human, financial and technical resources are rarely adequate, and there is almost always a need to develop fresh skills.

This is the conclusion reached by Rolph Payet, Minister of the Environment of the Republic of Seychelles and former president of the university of Seychelles, founded in 2009: "This is one of the youngest universities in the world. In the Seychelles we are totally committed to educating young people, and one of the biggest issues for us is developing environmental management. Without the necessary environmental quality, the Republic of Seychelles will never realise its potential. We are

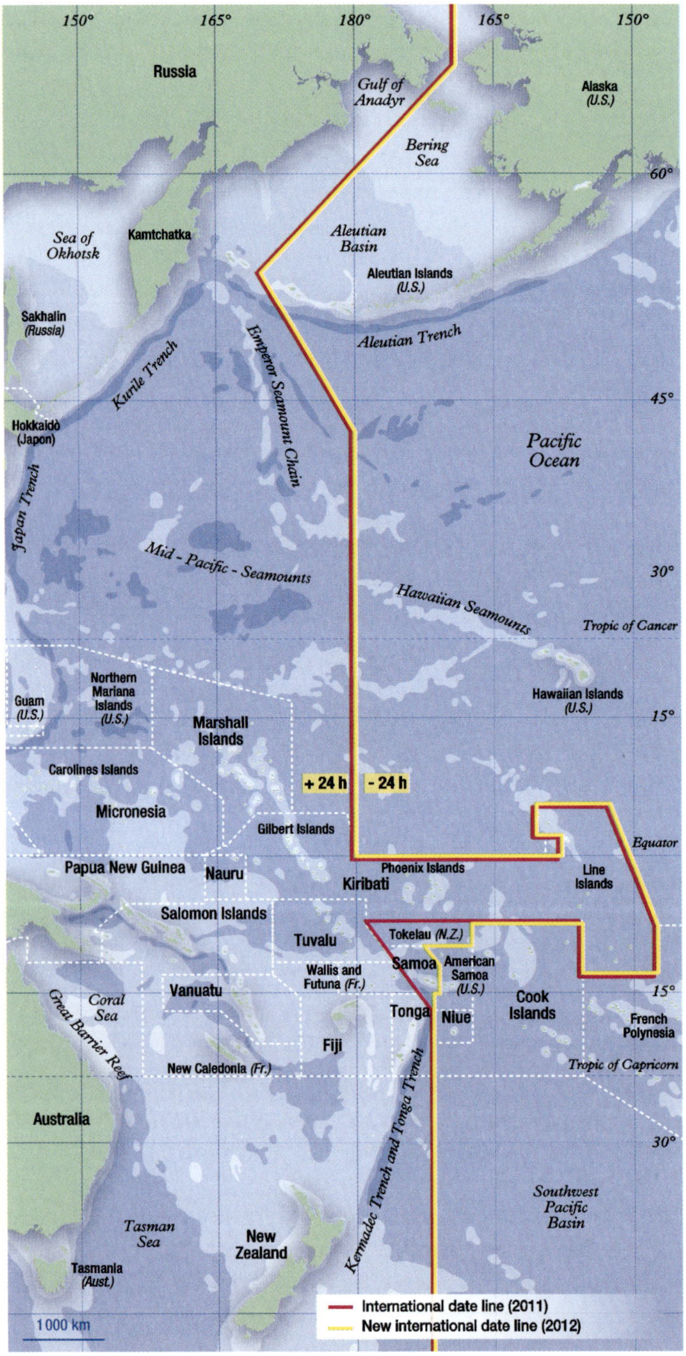

THE INTERNATIONAL DATELINE CUTS THROUGH THE PACIFIC CLOSE TO THE 180TH MERIDIAN. CLOSE TO THE LINE, TWO NEIGHBOURING COUNTRIES CAN BE SEPARATED BY AN ENTIRE DAY. IN 2012, AT THE REQUEST OF SAMOA, THE DATELINE WAS CHANGED TO REDUCE THE COUNTRY'S TIME GAP WITH AUSTRALIA AND NEW ZEALAND.

emphasising sustainable development because for us the very life-blood of the country is at stake. We've set up a masters in Geography and the Environment which includes courses on the environment in general, the tropical context, and forest management and its implications for water; water's a major issue on any island – you can't pipe it in from Africa, and on an island with no water there's no life. We've set up a national rainwater collection programme and experts from different parts of the region have been invited here to share their experiences with us. We're also going to improve management of fishing and marine resources generally, the coastline and our specific economic spheres."
Claude Colin, who was an attaché at the French Embassy in the Seychelles and a resident since 1998, is equally emphatic regarding the need for education and the development of local skills: "Initially I was a French teacher, then I began working at the embassy as coordinator of cooperative programmes between France and the Republic of Seychelles. Today development in the Seychelles means increasing skills that for the moment are limited, especially in the service sector. The opening of the university is part of this agenda, because the country needs properly trained executives. There are lots of small, private business ventures, notably in the trades and services – computers, for example – but the training isn't up to standard. We need more technicians for equipment repair and maintenance: in one recent case we had to call in diesel fitters from Mauritius!"

FROM NUTMEG TO NEW TECHNOLOGY

From an economic point of view certain island nations, such as the Bahamas and Malta, are relatively rich. The gross domestic product per head of population in the islands of the Caribbean and the Indian and Pacific oceans matches the average calculated by the World Bank and the International Monetary Fund; by contrast, the Comoros, Haiti and São Tomé and Príncipe suffer from extensive poverty and 12 island states are to be found on the United Nations list of least developed countries (LDCs). These disparities are explicable in terms of the islands' histories and their political, social and environmental situations.
The economic paths island states follow vary from one country to another. Many of them export agricultural products: sugar in Fiji, nutmeg in Grenada and bananas in Dominica are just three examples. In the Kiribati Islands, agriculture is almost entirely based on copra. But while exports often hinge on biodiversity, high transport costs and low productivity in comparison with large, continental countries hamper competitiveness. Many other island nations centre their economies on the ocean: aquaculture in Madagascar, fishing in the Seychelles, tourism in the Bahamas and the Maldives. In the Kiribatis and Tuvalu the sale of fishing licences for their economic zones represents 40% of the gross domestic product.

FOLLOWING DOUBLE PAGE: THE LOFOTEN ARCHIPELAGO IN THE NORTH ATLANTIC IS PART OF NORWAY.
ITS WATERS ARE RICH IN FISH, AND THE GREAT MAJORITY OF THE INHABITANTS ARE FISHERMEN.

TOP: ON THE INDONESIAN ISLAND OF BALI, VILLAGE WOMEN PREPARE BASKETS OF FISH FOR THE MARKET. ARTISANAL FISHING IS A LIVELIHOOD FOR A LARGE PART OF THE POPULATION IN ALMOST ALL THE WORLD'S INHABITED ISLANDS.

BOTTOM: LAND BEING LIMITED ON ISLANDS – AS HERE, ON MALTA IN THE MEDITERRANEAN – FARMING IS RARELY A LARGE-SCALE ACTIVITY.

Tourism, number two on the list of island industries, has been steadily expanding, to the point where, in many cases, it now represents the main source of foreign currency. In terms of gross domestic product it is running at 49% in Palau, 47% in the Cook Islands, 17% in Vanuatu and 13% in Fiji.[15] This state of affairs is not without its problems where resources and environmental damage are concerned (see page 169), but island tourism continues to offer considerable employment and income potential. As a geostrategic crossroads between Europe and Africa, Malta has opted for sea trade as its main economic platform. 15% of all Mediterranean traffic passes through its ports and with 1,500 ships flying its flag this small state has Europe's largest merchant marine fleet. There are, too, a number of islands that have become banking centres, using tax incentives to attract financial and other businesses. Sometimes, however, this has led them to become tax havens and hubs for the laundering of illegally earned money – hardly a context for sustainable economic development. Some island states have the good fortune to possess mineral assets: Jamaica exports bauxite, gypsum and limestone; Trinidad and Tobago and East Timor produce oil and natural gas; and the hydrocarbons, minerals and precious metals to be found at enormous depths in the exclusive economic zones of many island states may turn out to be a source of considerable wealth in the not so distant future. Other sectors attracting a great deal of interest include information technology, which facilitates communication with the outside world and encourages development of related services on the islands themselves. A number of island states, including Singapore, Cuba and Fiji, are currently working at forging a niche for themselves on the international IT scene.

SUSTAINABLE, INTEGRATED TERRITORIAL MANAGEMENT

In an island context of limited space being nibbled away by urbanisation and human activity, how is sufficient farmland to be found to meet the needs of a growing population? Some island countries have opted for creating new, artificial islands or cutting down their forests. And yet experts in the fields of the environment and economic and social development are now insisting more and more on the need to establish integrated approaches which take account not only of the interests of users of the natural setting – farmers, industrialists, foresters, fishermen, tour companies, etc. – but also of the preservation of that setting and its concomitant resources. Today new development strategies are being applied to these territories: forest protection and in some cases reforestation mean preservation of a protective green covering that prevents rainwater from simply washing away the top layer of fertile soil. The most striking anti-example is Madagascar, which has lost three-quarters of its forest cover in less than a century and become a distressing illustration of the ravages caused by mindless deforestation. With its high plateaux stripped bare, the

island's soil is gradually disappearing into its rivers and streams and thence into the sea, where it chokes the fragile coral along the coast. Fortunately preservation measures and awareness campaigns have slowed deforestation considerably – to a rate of only 0.5% of the territory in 2008.
If food security for island inhabitants is also to be maintained, sustainable forest management is vital: ways must be found of obtaining the necessary quantities of wood without lapsing back into the overharvesting of the past. Equally important are farming techniques that do not impoverish the soil, together with controlled use of fertilisers and insecticides. And in the interests of containing coastal erosion, certain island states are now striving to preserve the coral reefs that form natural barriers against the waves.
Traditional activities, of course, are a fundamental part of meeting islanders' needs, since they account for the greater part of their food and income. Upping consumption of imports to the detriment of local output makes no sense socially: it separates an island's population from time-honoured, revenue-producing pursuits and, moreover, imposes goods from the continent that are much more expensive. Marine and terrestrial biodiversity provides island dwellers with food, materials and medicine, while at the same time it is an ecological force for good, decontaminating the soil and structuring the water cycle. Preservation of nature's vitality and regeneration of flora and fauna are crucial in ensuring sustainable, equitable economic growth and improving quality of life for all. To help them succeed in the long term, management programmes for these natural resources are most effective when based on involvement of local communities: this can be seen in many protected areas in which villagers themselves apply the measures needed to forestall overexploitation (see page 141).

LEFT: RAISING PEARL OYSTERS IN POLYNESIA.
RIGHT: A MANGROVE REPLANTING OPERATION BY SHRIMP FARMERS IN MADAGASCAR.

THE OCEAN AS KINGDOM

VAST MARITIME SPACES

As a rule islands have a marine territory much, much larger than their land areas. The Republic of Seychelles, for example, possesses an exclusive economic zone (EEZ) bigger than France, Spain and Portugal combined: 1,336,559 square kilometres, as against a total land area of 455 square kilometres. Similarly, the Kiribatis have 3,441,810 square kilometres of sea and 802 square kilometres of land, a proportion of over 4000:1. The United Nations has estimated that the exclusive economic zones of the world's island states represent a sixth of the Earth's surface.

These sea zones are home to living resources that can be exploited by fishermen and are extremely promising in terms of biodiversity, as new substances with all sorts of research potential are being constantly discovered: molecules from marine animals – reef fauna, for instance – are rich in applications in the fields of health and industry. On the other hand, the mineral wealth of the sea floor – oil, gas, precious metals – attracts the attention of the major continental states, making it possible for islands to sell mining rights: already many island governments have seized this opportunity to finance development. The EEZs also represent a major strategic and military factor, in that they provide control of the shipping routes and passages currently used by 90% of international commodity transport. To cite one example, 80% of the oil consumed by Japan arrives by sea, just as many other countries count on sea transport for their raw materials. This helps us understand why countries in general claim marine spaces extending well beyond their actual coastlines.

LEFT: ARTISANAL FISHING PORT, MAHÉ, SEYCHELLES.
RIGHT: A EUROPEAN TUNA BOAT UNLOADS ITS CATCH IN THE INDUSTRIAL FISHING PORT IN MAHÉ, SEYCHELLES.

In the Seychelles life is concentrated along the shores and the economic activities of the 85,000 inhabitants are directly tied to the ocean, either as fishing or tourism: "We have a great variety of fish species," says Rolph Payet, "and we've set up mechanisms for protecting these marine resources. Fishing provides us with food and we export tuna as a way of boosting the economy, creating jobs and facilitating development. Without fish there would be no Seychelles and without the Seychelles

humanity would lose a pearl of great price. Tourism is economically significant too: it brings in foreign currency and helps us create the infrastructures needed for development and greater receptivity to the world at large."

In addition there is an interconnection between the dynamism and health of these various industries: well-managed fishing keeps restaurants supplied at the same time as it protects the well-being of the seafloor – which in turn is a drawing card for the tourists who come to swim, dive, and admire whales, turtles and all sorts of other marine life. In the Caribbean, for example, sea-related activities – fishing, tourism, sailing – accounted for 40% of the region's gross domestic product in 2010.

And so the destiny of the world's islands is tied to the sea. Their marine heritage is an enormous asset and a vital resource for a large proportion of residents. It also,

EROSION DUE TO DEFORESTATION HAS DRASTIC CONSEQUENCES, INCLUDING LOSS OF FARMLAND AND SOIL DEGRADATION. RIVER-BORNE SEDIMENTS FLOW INTO THE SEA AND STIFLE MARINE LIFE, AS HERE IN THE BETSIBOKA RIVER IN MADAGASCAR.

however, represents a responsibility: how are such small countries to manage such vast marine areas? Preserving the environment and developing the means of surveillance necessary to prevent overexploitation, illegal or uncontrolled fishing and the plundering of the seabed is a major challenge.

A FISHERMAN'S LIFE

On most islands fishing is among the principal economic activities. Artisanal fishing feeds local markets and provides a living for numerous families. In the developing tropical countries 60% of all food comes from the sea, and sustainable management of this asset is absolutely vital.
Lucie Ah-Kong is one of the Seychelles' rare professional fisherwomen. When her grown-up children moved out she chose the occupation for sheer love of fishing: "A year and a half ago my husband and I bought our boat, and the two of us work aboard right through the fishing season, from October to February. Depending on the state of the sea and the boat – and the quantity of fish! – we set out for seven or nine days at a time. We fish for *bourgeois*,[16] working *à la palangrotte*,[17] and we

AS AN INVALUABLE SOURCE OF KNOWLEDGE ABOUT THE NATURAL ENVIRONMENT, TRADITIONAL KNOWLEDGE HANDED DOWN BY THE ELDERS CAN MAKE A DECISIVE CONTRIBUTION TO ITS PRESERVATION.

come back once we've caught around 500 kilograms of fish. I'd always wanted to be a fisherwoman and go to sea. I'm really excited when we're getting the boat and the lines ready, and when we're out there – especially if the weather's calm – I forget all my problems. I never really want to come ashore again."

Island fishermen are absolutely convinced of the need for sustainable management of their resources, and all sorts of strategies have been tested. The Seychelles fishing community has united as the Seychelles Hook and Line Fishermen's Association and its members have set up a certification system that guarantees fish quality and observation of environmental standards. The system gives their product recognition on both the international and the domestic markets, and in particular in local restaurants catering to tourists. As association president Joe Dingwall recounts, "Certified fishing was introduced in 2008 as a way of being able to export without our fish being mixed in with fish from elsewhere. Seychelles red snapper tastes better than red snapper from Asia and other places, and it's more expensive." The snapper is caught at a depth of 30–50 metres, using special hooks that protect the environment by excluding undersize specimens – which are left to become adults and reproduce – and such other marine creatures as turtles. On board the boat the fish intended for local consumption are cleaned and packed in ice. "We take 5 or 6 metric tons of red snapper per year," says Joe Dingwall, "but only 10% are exported to Europe. The certification brings us a better price. But fishermen here don't restrict themselves to red snapper. The season finishes in May, and then we turn to other species. We're also thinking of extending certification to blue-green snapper, the various *carangues*, and the spangled emperor. Certification hasn't really changed fishermen's habits, but the fish sells better now. I encourage people to eat certified fish because it's healthier and our fishing methods are sustainable. Looking to the future, we'd prefer not to have to show our kids a book and say, 'Look, that's an Emperor Red Snapper, you used to find them here but there aren't any left now.' Instead of that, we want things to continue."

As part of the venture Berty Hoareau, a member of the association, recently went to France to meet restaurant owners and promote the Seychelles certification system. Partnerships were set up with likeminded associations in Brittany, with a view to exchanges of techniques and skills. This kind of initiative is a real motor for small-scale fishing, provided you can get the necessary backing from the consumer: this means it is especially important to get the message across in importing countries, and this has to be done via awareness campaigns all along the chain from the initial buyer to the consumer.

INDUSTRIAL FISHING: A CRUCIAL SECTOR

Industrialised fishing boosts the economic development of the countries involved and can provide jobs on a large scale. Today 55% of the world's tuna catch – estimated at well over 2 billion dollars per annum – comes from small island countries in the

Pacific. In the Maldives fishing is a modern, highly-developed industry that employs over 10% of the workforce, represents the main source of income for 20% of the population, and accounts for 98% of the value of all exports.[18] On the other hand, apart from a few fruits and vegetables, the Maldives import virtually all the rest of their food. And certain island states actually import more fish products than they export: tourist-related demand is high and coastal waters are sometimes overfished or polluted, as is the case in several Caribbean countries.

Sometimes the bottom can drop out of a fishing industry with no warning, and when this happens an entire segment of the island's economy collapses, endangering the country's stability and food security. This has led to plans for integrated, long-term management mechanisms for fish resources – changes that were well overdue since, according to the United Nations Food and Agriculture Organisation (FAO), in 2007 28% of world fish stocks were overexploited, exhausted or in a recovery phase; 52% were fully exploited; and only 20% were underexploited. A large part of the overfishing problem lies in the failure to adequately combat illegal, unregulated and "black economy" fishing, believed to represent some 30% of all catches.

In the 1960s catches of tuna in the Maldives were running at 20,000 metric tons, a figure whose steady increase peaked at 186,000 metric tons in 2005. Since then catches have diminished,[19] in part because measures including selective fishing equipment have been put into effect. Because tuna are migratory species, an intergovernmental commission had to be set up to manage the fish population from one region to another. Based on cooperation between its member countries, the commission imposes quotas and fishing regulations to optimise use of existing stocks while ensuring sustainable preservation. In the Indian Ocean and its adjacent areas the different species of tuna are managed by the Indian Ocean Tuna Commission (IOTC).

Island states wanting to make the most of their marine heritage do not always have the financial means to develop a large-scale fishing industry, complete with port infrastructures, ships and processing plants. As a result exploitation is often left to foreign countries, which the host country licenses to fish in its waters. Income from the sale of licences allows island states to diversify their sources of revenue without the need for significant investment. The presence of industrial-scale foreign fishing vessels also gives rise to development of port activities, as is explained by Jan Robinson, head of research at the Seychelles Fishing Authority (SFA): "The fishing sector is extremely important, as industrial fishing generates both jobs and revenue. Tuna-fishing licences are granted to French and Spanish trawlers, for example, but most importantly of all, the ships using the port of Victoria generate a substantial segment of our economic activity." Dozens of enormous trawlers spend a large part of the year in the Seychelles and their crews are part of local life. In addition, a tuna processing plant built in the port provides jobs for local workers.

Fishing is not just a variant on farming. The resources are taken directly from their setting, which means that certain factors have to be taken into account by island

communities when it comes to developing this crucial sector: overfishing; variations in stock levels, whether natural or due to climate change; the difficulty of keeping the sea under surveillance and a lack of the necessary facilities; fluctuations within the global economy and their effects on transport and commodity costs. Given these numerous challenges, mobilisation of all involved and responsible management represent direct, major contributions to ongoing preservation of fishing as a stable economic activity.

FARMING THE SEA

The shrimp has been called Madagascar's "pink gold". Both the wild coastal version and those raised on farms are mainly exported to Europe, and together with tourism they make up one of the country's main sources of foreign currency. The sector provides a living for people settled on the coast and in the estuaries and mangrove areas, which do not lend themselves to other kinds of farming. In 2007 shrimp fishing and aquaculture accounted for some 10,000 direct and 40,000 indirect jobs, as well as representing a hands-on food source for the local people. In other words the shrimp industry, in its various forms, is part of the fight against poverty and a key factor in the nation's future.

Ocean shrimping in Madagascar involves some eighty industrial trawlers and forty small, privately owned boats. The sea also offers a livelihood to the thousands of fishermen in traditional, non-motorised pirogues, responsible for close to a third of the

ISLANDS ARE THE FIRST TO SUFFER FROM CHANGES IN THE MARINE ENVIRONMENT: POLLUTION, RISES IN WATER TEMPERATURE, LOSS OF BIODIVERSITY. CLOSE STUDY CAN HELP WITH ANTICIPATING MAJOR ENVIRONMENTAL UPSETS.

country's total catch. The industry is bound by strict ecological criteria: joint development zones known as ZACs have been created, together with a "Code of Mutual Respect", and shrimping is now restricted to specific times of the year. The special nets used avoid the taking of undersized specimens and are equipped with escape systems for turtles, dolphins and big fish. Reduction of the number of diesel engines on shrimping ships and the establishment of processing plants near the unloading zones have brought carbon emissions down; these measures were talked over and adopted by the producers themselves within the framework of the GAPCM, the Shrimp Aquaculturalists and Fishers Group of Madagascar, before being ratified by the government. Because large-scale erosion on the island has driven many small farmers to turn to the sea for food, there is now greater pressure on marine resources. Water pollution and deterioration of the reefs have also undermined marine ecosystems and shrimp are becoming less numerous in Madagascan waters. The need to avoid excessive dependence on wild shrimp populations has led to the development of aquaculture, characterised by low-density production – 30 specimens to the square metre, as opposed to 300 in Asia – and organic feeding, both of which minimise the practice's environmental impact. All refuse is processed to avoid pollution and programmes of mangrove re-planting are already under way. These measures give Madagascan shrimps an incomparable taste, but their implementation costs money and this pushes prices up. If they are to hold their own on the market in the context of today's economic crisis, Madagascar's shrimp need consumers ready to accept the cost of their producers' environmental and social agendas.

Aquaculture programmes are now to be found on practically all the world's islands. In Polynesia, for example, the long-established trade in nacre, or mother of pearl, suddenly boomed in the 1960s, and oyster populations dropped radically. Steps were taken to restrict the taking of oysters, with the Fisheries Department and private enterprise joining forces to try farming techniques based on the traditional model used in Japan and China. The spats – the fertilised oyster eggs – are harvested, then placed on collectors and attached to long ropes which remain in the water until the oysters have grown. Then the "graft" takes place, with a fragment of another mollusc being introduced into the shell. To defend itself against this foreign body, the oyster coats it with nacre and the pearl is born. Polynesian production of black pearls, based on *Pinctada margaritifera*, the Black-lip Oyster, makes up 90% of the world's output. In cash terms Tahiti pearls represent three-quarters of these islands' exports, as well as providing several thousand jobs on the atolls. The pearl industry has its problems, however, in the form of unpredictable results and the need for certification to counter competition from inferior products. With this in mind a process of reorganisation is now under way.

Pearl-raising allows its practitioners to become "farmers of the sea" and live off the ocean's resources without detriment to wild populations. Marine aquaculture,

SUSTAINABLE MANAGEMENT OF THE PRODUCTS OF THE SEA INVOLVES BETTER KNOWLEDGE OF MARINE SPECIES AND THEIR BIOLOGY.

TOP LEFT: FISHMARKET, VICTORIA, SEYCHELLES.
TOP RIGHT: TUNA FARM, MEDITERRANEAN.
BOTTOM: SHRIMP FARM, MADAGASCAR.

ISLAND COUNTRIES HAVE REALISED THE NEED FOR LONG-TERM PROTECTION OF THE FISH IN THEIR TERRITORIAL WATERS. THEY ARE NOW ORGANISING MANAGEMENT OF THIS CRUCIAL ECONOMIC RESOURCE AT REGIONAL LEVEL.

however, is a technically complex business, involving close familiarity with the life cycle of the species concerned, provision of appropriate nourishment during the various stages of the process, protection against disease and prevention of pollution and damage to the breeding environment. This makes it difficult to set in motion and also means that output remains limited. Very few establishments bring in revenue that is significant in national terms. Nonetheless, numerous initiatives for repopulation of reefs and creation of small pearl farms on a village scale are taking shape now, with considerable promise for the future (see page 151).

ENSURING SECURITY: A MAJOR ISSUE

ECONOMIC STABILITY

Small islands are in something of a predicament, as Dessima Williams, Grenada's ambassador to the United Nations and until 2011 president of the Alliance of Small Island States, points out: "Their cultures and societies are dynamic and pioneering, but almost all of them have poverty and unemployment rates of around 20–30%. We small island developing states lack the means to adequately finance sustainable development and cope with climate change. We are small countries faced with a monumental debt that in many cases is more than 100% of our gross domestic product."
Independence is not something that happens solely at the economic level. How can we ensure the security of small island nations, which are sometimes split on ethnic or religious lines and have limited means of self-defence? Vulnerable to the dangers of all kinds of trafficking, they sometimes end up as hubs for the drug trade, money laundering and other illegal activities. Most of the world's tax havens are on islands, although a number of states recently targeted by the international community have undertaken to respect the regulations regarding exchange of fiscal data. Other islands find themselves being courted by continental powers for strategic reasons, for their natural or mineral wealth, or for their votes at the United Nations – votes, which can sometimes be negotiated in terms of financial aid… As a means of ensuring the stability of these states and countering illegal activities which can threaten their own security, certain continental powers offer logistical support in return for a commitment to tackling home-grown disorder and corruption. In some cases these powerful countries also finance development projects in the fields of education, health, economic growth and preservation of the environment.

In the Seychelles, former French embassy attaché Claude Colin analyses the government's handling of economic problems as follows: "Between 1997–2008 the Seychelles went through a difficult time economically. The external debt was very high, the Seychelles Rupee was overvalued, and it was hard for the country to borrow. In 2008, with the help of the International Monetary Fund, a major programme of reform set out to renegotiate both the debt and the value of the local currency. The programme seems to have worked, and today the government is taking steps to make sure that the budget remains balanced. Before the reforms, the country's economically wobbly state made foreigners loath to invest there, but the big hotel companies have now come back and the 'offshore' sector has sprouted, offering tax advantages to companies willing to set up house there. At the same time the Seychelles are not a 'grey area' and investors are encouraged to expand their activities, notably in the tourism field."

PIRATES: A THREAT TO THE SECURITY OF ISLAND STATES

For several years now a steady escalation in piracy at sea has been a major problem for island states, especially those in the Indian Ocean. Based in Somalia, these pirates are a threat to all kinds of navigation, from big fishing boats to small pleasure craft; in addition scientific, oceanographic and hydrocarbon research missions have been slowed down and even cancelled because of the potential danger. The increase in the number of incidents has forced states to take elaborate precautionary measures in the region. Claude Colin points out that piracy has been costing the Seychelles up to 4% of its gross domestic product in 2010, as it is extremely difficult to keep the whole of this vast marine area under surveillance.

The key sectors affected by piracy are tourism, fishing and imports. The outlying islands are now no-go areas for tourists and a number of cruise companies have found themselves on the verge of forced shut-down. Supplies of gas and oil have also been affected. "However," says Claude Colin, "the government has resolved to combat the problem, via joint action with the coast guard and aid from Europe, the United States, India, Japan and other countries. The big fishing companies have called in private security forces, and in the case of French concerns have been given assistance by the army as well."

THE PERILS OF OVEREXPLOITATION

Preservation of the environment is also a matter of individual safety in small island territories. Overexploitation or degradation of an island's main resource can have drastic consequences for the population as a whole: loss of jobs, a fall in foreign currency revenue, destruction of the natural setting, etc. The nation may even find itself bankrupt, as was the case of the world's smallest state, the island of Nauru (see box): here we had one of the most spectacular examples of massive environmental breakdown, brought on in just a few years by overexploitation of the island's minerals. Whence the importance of sustainable, long-term management of natural resources as something vital for our planet as a whole and its islands in particular.

When an entire economy has been adversely affected, one way of getting back on the road to lasting economic and social development can be international aid and cooperation between countries facing the same kinds of difficulties. Economic diversification, investment in sustainable modes of production and establishment of sectors conducive to food and energy autonomy are thus urgent development concerns for island states today.

NAURU: REBUILDING THE FUTURE

In the *New York Times* of 18 July 2011, under the heading "A Sinking Feeling", Marcus Stephen, who would remain president of the Republic of Nauru until November of that year, launched a moving appeal to the world:

"I forgive you if you have never heard of my country. At just 8 square miles, about a third of the size of Manhattan, and located in the southern Pacific Ocean, Nauru appears as merely a pinpoint on most maps – if it is not missing entirely in a vast expanse of blue. But make no mistake; we are a sovereign nation, with our own language, customs and history dating back 3,000 years."

The Republic of Nauru is lost in the middle of the Pacific, 2,000 kilometres from Papua-New Guinea. A single road circles the island, whose 21 square kilometres are home to 9,000 Nauruan speakers, the distant descendants of Polynesians, Micronesians and Melanesians. When Europeans – among them the English explorer John Fearn – first landed here in 1798, they found what seemed a paradise, and named it Pleasant Island.

In the early twentieth century came the discovery of phosphate. Germans and British began excavating all over the island for this precious ingredient for fertiliser. When Nauru became independent in 1968 it was one of the richest countries in the world, but this time of plenty was not to last: by 1990 the phosphate was gone and the island transformed into a vast strip mine on which nothing new would grow. A few dubious real estate ventures apart, the government had made no long-term investments and by 1994 the country was bankrupt. The holdings of the Nauru Phosphate Royalties Trust, in charge of administering the income from phosphate mining, dropped from 1.3 billion Australian dollars in 1991 to 138 million in 2002. With the economic collapse came social crisis: no longer able to import the consumer goods they were almost totally dependent on, Nauruans lapsed into desperate poverty.

NAURU, THE SMALLEST COUNTRY IN THE WORLD, HAS SEEN ITS TERRITORY DEVASTATED BY INTENSIVE PHOSPHATE MINING.

WITH ONLY 9,000 INHABITANTS, THE REPUBLIC OF NAURU IS A TINY STATE LOST IN THE MID-PACIFIC. ITS NEAREST NEIGHBOURS ARE THE SMALL ISLAND OF BANABA AND THE KIRIBATI ARCHIPELAGO, RESPECTIVELY 300 AND 600 KILOMETRES AWAY.

Many of them were ill from an over-rich diet poorly suited to the Polynesian metabolism: 78% were obese and 40% diabetic. With a traumatised state on its hands, the government tried to turn the island first into a tax haven, then into a detention centre for illegal immigrants.

Today the Nauruans are setting about rebuilding their nation. International aid is helping the country stay on its feet, but the reconstruction process is probably going to be longer than that period of ephemeral wealth. A search is on for precious metals in the deep waters of the Pacific and the islanders are turning to fishing and the creation of renewable energy as tools for a new future. Sustainable development and environmental preservation are now key aspects of government policy and programmes are underway for restoration of the land devastated by mining.

"I forgive you if you have never heard of Nauru," wrote Marcus Stephen, "but you will not forgive yourselves if you ignore our story."

Outpost Islands

"Maybe it's because we're small, but we see the big issues very clearly," commented Thomas Tillman, then prime minister of Grenada, in New York in 2009. For decades now island residents have been faced with questions of water supply, refuse handling, energy production and social and economic development in a context complicated by globalization pressures and worldwide environmental degradation. In coming up with strategies adapted to their territories and communities, they are suggesting tactical avenues for the planet's future.

GUARDIANS OF THE OCEAN

LIKE LIGHTHOUSES

In the same speech to the United Nations in New York, given during a meeting for the Action Programme for Sustainable Development in Small Island Developing States, Thomas Tillman also asserted that "one of the characteristics of small island states is their unique relationship with the World Ocean." No question, this relation is an intimate and essential one: like lighthouses, islands are outposts for continental landmasses and the first witnesses of the sea's changing temper.

Rolph Payet, Minister of the Environment of the Republic of Seychelles, is equally conscious of this special link with the sea: "The Seychelles' marine heritage is the life of the islands, the life of their people, and my life. When you grow up with the sea, amid dolphins and turtles, you learn to appreciate the fragility of this environment – and its beauty and complexity as well. I'm a diver, and beneath the surface you can see the impacts of poaching, global warming and pollution. When I saw the coral bleaching I even stopped diving for a time."

The ocean is indispensable to islanders' survival, but its balance is being disturbed in all sorts of ways: uncontrolled coastal development, pollution by agricultural and industrial chemicals, oil spills, waste water, rising temperatures, etc. Often the sources of these problems are far from the islands themselves: everything ends up in the sea and ocean pollution has no nationality and knows no borders. To cite one example, in 2003, during an expedition to Kure, an isolated island northwest of Hawaii, the explorer/filmmaker Jean-Michel Cousteau, son of the famous Jacques-Yves Cousteau, found the shores littered with plastic from all over the world. A point

PREVIOUS DOUBLE PAGE: CORAL REEF RESTORATION PROGRAMMES ARE NOW UNDER WAY IN MANY TROPICAL REGIONS. "CUTTINGS" OF HEALTHY CORAL ARE REPLANTED IN AFFECTED AREAS, AS HERE IN THE GLORIEUSES ISLANDS.

of convergence for all the currents in the North Pacific, the region acts as a kind of immense whirlpool, sucking in waste from everywhere. The debris gets coated with fish spawn, then eaten by albatrosses and regurgitated as food for their young; and the young die. Marine mammals, fish and invertebrates are also poisoned by heavy metals scattered by the currents. These disruptions of the environment's physical characteristics – temperature, for instance, or acidity level – can have drastic consequences for marine ecosystems all over the world.

And so human activity and lifestyles in big developed countries impact directly on island economies. Surrounded by water, islands largely depend on the ocean: they are the first to suffer when it malfunctions and by sending out messages to the world they play a fundamental part in the lives of all of us. It is vital for humanity, then, that we study, understand and find ways of preserving them. All sorts of initiatives are already underway, but if islands are to adapt to current upheavals in their marine environments, they need international backing in terms of finances and skills. At grassroots level they are coming up with research and development solutions, which we are all going to need in the more or less long term.

ON MOUNTAINOUS VOLCANIC ISLANDS – AS HERE IN THE COMOROS –SPACE IS DESPERATELY SHORT.
TOWNS AND INDUSTRIES DEVELOP ALONG THE COAST.

COMMUNITY INVOLVEMENT

Islands have a strong agricultural tradition: in every village gardens provide the fruit and vegetables that form the basis of the local diet. On many atolls the inhabitants combine reef fishing with cultivating tubers, including taro, and harvesting coconuts. For these sea people the wealth of the ocean is a dominant factor, and many island development projects focus on sound management of coastal resources

by shoreline village communities. In New York, at a pre-Rio+20[20] meeting held in September 2011 by the Global Ocean Forum,[21] Fijian ambassador Peter Thomson reminded the world, “For the Pacific SIDs (Small Island Developing States), given our dependence on the health of marine ecosystems, urgent progress is needed to implement existing commitments, to address new and emerging issues and to solidify the nexus between ocean management and sustainable development that is lacking in the international framework.” By 2010, 83% of Small Island States had already created Marine Protected Areas (MPAs) in their territorial waters, the aim being a balance between human activity and long-term preservation of their marine ecology.
This approach has been used in Fiji, where a large part of the population lives off artisanal coastal fishing. The men go out to sea, while the women harvest shellfish

WOMEN AND CHILDREN OFTEN HARVEST SEA PRODUCE ALONG THE SHORELINE: SHELLFISH, SEA URCHINS AND OTHER SMALL CREATURES ARE EATEN IN THE VILLAGE OR SOLD ON LOCAL MARKETS.

including the andara, an edible bivalve. During the 1990s the Fijians noticed that the andara was becoming increasingly rare, as overexploitation of marine resources led to degradation of the reef. This was happening in spite of the fact that like many islands in the Pacific, Fiji has a system of customary fishing rights based on *qoliqoli*, zones administered by the village chiefs. As a means of letting fish populations re-establish themselves, villagers observe taboos regarding fishing areas and reproduction periods. There are 385 *qoliqoli* in Fiji and this traditional system serves as the basis for such modern marine management tools as the Locally Managed Marine Areas (LMMA), reserves overseen by local communities. In the small village of Ucunivanua, on the west coast of Viti Levu, the creation of an LMMA some years ago brought about the return of certain species and a repopulation of the surrounding marine areas. The villagers live off the produce of the sea and families gain extra income by selling the surplus in Suva, the capital.

Reserves of this kind are now appearing in many other parts of the Pacific, and elsewhere: in the Solomon Islands, the Cook Islands and Vanuatu, for example. In these instances, too, traditional taboo zones already existed as a means of preserving resources not only in the restricted fishing areas but in the surrounding waters as well. Advancing modernisation had led to their abandonment, but they are now being looked into again by the inhabitants and those in charge of managing fishing and the environment. With the backing of NGOs and local bodies, projects have been set up to combine development with autonomy.

In New Caledonia, for example, a program backed by the World Wildlife Fund (WWF) has successfully reintroduced the giant clam on the northeast coast. This large mollusc is traditionally eaten by the inhabitants, who harvest it when it is three or four years old. The local variety, *Hippopus hippopus*, known as the Bear Paw or Horse's Hoof Clam, does not cling to the reef and is easily captured, the result being a marked decline in the population. In 2009 a hundred of them raised on a farm on the west coast were introduced into a Marine Protected Area where fishing is prohibited. Local Kanaka tribes were involved in the project, which was monitored by local management committees with the backing of fishing technicians. When the clams reproduced, eggs were taken and used to refertilise another part of the reef for later fishing purposes. The aim of the organisers is to adapt the programme to local requirements: for example, are the clams eaten regularly, or only during traditional celebrations? This cooperative effort involving local communities, the relevant environmental body and an NGO is an excellent example of a sustainable development project aimed at meeting inhabitants' long-term needs.

THE LIVELIHOODS OF 500 MILLION PEOPLE AROUND THE WORLD, MANY OF THEM ISLANDERS, DEPEND AT LEAST IN PART ON THE CORAL REEFS WHICH SUPPLY FOOD AND WORK AND PROTECT THE COASTS. SOUND HEALTH FOR CORAL REEFS IS A BASIC TOOL FOR FIGHTING POVERTY.

FOLLOWING DOUBLE PAGE: THE LIMESTONE CHELBACHEB ISLANDS IN REPUBLIC OF PALAU (MICRONESIA, PACIFIC) ARE HOME TO SALT LAKES INHABITED BY THOUSANDS OF NON-STINGING JELLYFISH. THE GOVERNMENT HAS CREATED A HUGE MARINE PROTECTED AREA TO PRESERVE ITS REMARKABLE HERITAGE.

EVEN WHEN SITUATED AT GREAT DISTANCES FROM THE CONTINENTS, ISLANDS CAN BE AFFECTED BY POLLUTION PRODUCED BY HUMANS ELSEWHERE: TRANSPORTED BY SEA CURRENTS AND THE WIND, TOXIC PARTICLES ARE ABSORBED BY ANIMALS AND THEN ENTER THE FOOD CHAIN.

NETWORKING MARINE PROTECTED AREAS

At the Rio Earth Summit in 1992, the participating nations agreed on the importance of natural environments for humanity and the need for managing them sustainably. With a view to improved knowledge and preservation of coral reefs – considered among the planet's richest ecosystems – in 1995 the United States founded the International Coral Reef Initiative (ICRI). France, which has an enormous reef heritage in its overseas territory, works on management and protection through the Initiative Française pour les Récifs Coralliens (IFRECOR), a national offshoot of ICRI, but is also active at the international level. Veterinarian and marine biology researcher Eric Clua coordinates Coral Reef InitiativeS for the Pacific (CRISP) initiated by France. CRISP partners all sorts of organisations in promoting protection and long-term management of these uniquely indispensable assets. Financed by the French Fund for the World Environment (FFEM) and the French Development Agency (AFD), this program, established in 2004–11, has supported many integrated development projects for islands; its originality lies in the fact that it did not involve creating yet another body, providing instead financial resources and networking facilities for partner bodies already at work in the region. Its aim is also to ensure coordination in the fields of development and science by combining input from biology, ecology, economy, sociology, anthropology and law.

In Vanuatu CRISP has aided the creation of marine protected areas. "What's really interesting here," says Eric Clua, "is the villages' very real determination to create their own marine protected areas. There's one for every village. But there's also a determination to set networking in motion very quickly. This is the case, for example, in the north of the island of Efate, where twelve villages are already exchanging experiences and so making economies of scale. This is where CRISP is really valuable: not only can it draw on this networking for the rest of Vanuatu, it can also export it to see what happens in other places like Fiji or the Solomon Islands. It's in this context of added value and interchange of experience that it plays its role of regional vector to the full. It's not a matter of reinventing the wheel every time, but of promoting workable solutions that have already proved themselves elsewhere."

Monitoring the Vanuatu reserves is handled by the Foundation of South Pacific People (FSP), which brings ten countries together to coordinate community programs. Its role is to increase people's technical know-how, and this has been done by sending an extension worker to each village to identify the problems posed by marine resource management. The resultant analyses have led to a management and action plan overseen by the extension worker, who makes regular visits to each marine protected area. Monitoring of the reef is carried out by the inhabitants, who look after their undersea

IN BIODIVERSITY TERMS CORAL REEFS ARE THE EQUIVALENT OF TROPICAL FORESTS.
CORAL FARM IN VANUATU (TOP LEFT),
GIANT TRIDACNA CLAM (TOP RIGHT),
CORAL (BOTTOM LEFT),
GORGONIAN (BOTTOM RIGHT).

BECAUSE THEY ABSORB 70 TO 90% OF WAVE IMPACT, BARRIER REEFS PROTECT THE SHORELINE AGAINST EROSION.

garden as if it were a garden on land. No fishing or harvesting is allowed and fragments of living coral are placed on the reef to grow. Because these preservation programmes produce rapid, visible results – the coral builds up, the fish and shellfish return – fishermen and village leaders are soon won over. In Vanuatu the green snail, a mollusc 30 centimetres long and considered sacred by the local people, had all but vanished because of overharvesting; but in the wake of a reintroduction programme it has come back in force to recolonise the reef, to the great relief of the inhabitants. Chief Mormor of the village of Mangalilu is especially pleased: "My father and grandfather used to go fishing over there all the time and bring back endless quantities of green snails. I was a kid then, and I remember how we used to export them by the sack-load. The boats would come in and pick them up. But then they disappeared, down to the very last one. We're delighted by this reintroduction operation run by the fisheries department. It's very important for the people here."

LITTLE COUNTRIES, BIG AMBITIONS

Situated east of the Philippines, the Palau Archipelago has a richly diverse marine heritage underpinning its tourism and other significant economic activities. In 2003 the government backed the creation of a network with the Protected Area Network Act (PAN ACT), which designated 28 protected areas. Visitors from abroad contribute to the network's upkeep by paying a $15 tax at the airport when they leave the country. In 2009 Palau, whose marine territory is as big as France, declared that territory the world's first shark sanctuary: as long as appropriate surveillance can be effected, these waters will offer 135 endangered species, including the big hammerhead and leopard sharks, a refuge from fishing. At present the country lacks the necessary number of patrol boats, but is counting on the ban as a tool for deterrence. The Kiribati Islands are likewise investing in sound marine management. In 2006 this little republic in the Pacific set up the largest marine protected area in the world: 408,250 square kilometres – as big as California – which represent 12% of the national territory. In a zone whose waters can be as much as 6,000 metres deep, this is one of the planet's last intact coral archipelagos, and was given Unesco World Heritage listing in 2010. Kiribati president Anote Tong stated at the time, "For millennia, we have been an ocean people, depending on its many gifts and resources for our survival, but we believe its treasures are to be protected and shared for the long-term benefit of people everywhere. In this regard the Phoenix Islands Protected Area is our gift to humanity."[22]

OCEAN ECOLOGY AND THE FIGHT AGAINST POVERTY

Studies have been carried out to evaluate the economic effectiveness of Marine Protected Area (MPA): scientific fishing experiments indicate that a village close to an MPA catches 8 to 10 kilograms of fish per hour, with the quantity gradually dropping to 3 kilograms per hour as you move away. Catches nourish local populations, of course, but sales of the surplus can also bring in extra revenue.

To compensate for the economic loss caused by the ban on fishing within the reserve, other methods of making the most of marine resources have been developed. Tourism, for example, depends on a healthy environment and an interestingly diverse fauna, and visitors are attracted by nature in its wild state and the possibility of seeing turtles and other iconic marine life; so integrating preservation into tourism and other economic spheres is crucial to sound long-term reef management. In Vanuatu agreements have been reached with some reserves for profits from tourism to be divided into three parts: a third each for the accommodation establishment, the local community and the environmental management committee, which feeds the money back into MPA maintenance.

In the Solomon Islands CRISP-backed experiments collect scraps of coral broken off during storms and cultivate it in the lagoons for a year. With the aid of the WWF and government bodies, a private company has been set up to collect cultivated corals in villages all over the islands; the refrigerated fragments are taken by boat to Honiara, the capital, where exporters package them and send them to the United States for the fish-tank and aquarium trade. The fragments are sold when they have grown to some 10 centimetres long and the "coral farmers" sell an average of 20 to 60 a month – a profit of around $100.

Another, particularly inventive step towards replacement income for local communities was taken in French Polynesia some years ago, then extended to the Pacific and Indian oceans. This involved providing fish specimens for the aquarium market without damaging the environment. Many thousands of fish are caught for this lucrative market, which represents millions of dollars per year. Often they are taken with coarse nets that damage their gills, and brought to the surface without decompression, so that many of them die. This makes Eric Clua extremely angry: "It's a mad rush for money that excludes all precautions. A great waste economically – and ecologically as well." Sometimes divers in diving suits catch the fish with hand-nets, so as to avoid harming them: this raises the survival rate, but still diminishes reef populations. One remedy is a CRISP project backed by the French Fund for the World Environment (FFEM): reef fish larvae are taken at the passages between the lagoon and the ocean, using appropriate nets (see box, page 154). This gives fishermen an alternative to catching adult specimens in their

FOLLOWING DOUBLE PAGE: A HUMPBACK WHALE BALLET IN THE BLUE OCEAN DEPTHS. VARIOUS ASSOCIATIONS ARE WORKING WITH ECO-VOLUNTEERS TO STUDY AND PROTECT THESE CREATURES.

natural setting. The technique is now being used by private operators on several Indian Ocean islands – Mauritius, Madagascar, La Réunion – and in the Pacific, in the Solomons, Fiji and French Polynesia. This harvesting of larvae is often combined with such other initiatives as turtle reintroduction and coral reimplantation, all of which contribute to keeping the sea in good health. In French Polynesia sustainably captured reef fish larvae are used to "seed" the coral gardens in the artificial lagoons of the big luxury hotels; and this in turn earns the hotels ecotourism certification points.

BABY FISH FOR THE AQUARIUM TRADE

Every year lagoon fish congregate near the reef passages to reproduce and lay. Once hatched, the tiny larvae grow in the open sea, where there are fewer predators than in the lagoon, and some of them set off to colonise other islands. Between one and three months later some 10% of them come back towards the island in a post-larval state: no longer larvae, but not yet young fish. Under normal conditions only one larva in every 100,000 will reach adulthood, most of them falling victim to predators.

So, since they are almost certainly doomed, why not capture some of them before they move back into the lagoon? Using very fine nets, the fishermen collect them in the natural entrance to the lagoon, then transport them to fish farms for sorting according to species and size. Some will be sold on the aquarium market, others will be raised to adulthood then sold as food. Others still will be used to repopulate the lagoon. This approach is backed up by awareness campaigns urging aquarists to opt for these small fish in preference to adults from areas where destructive, unsustainable fishing techniques are used.

In France, for example, at Nausicaá, the National Marine Centre in Boulogne-sur-Mer, 80% of the fish in the enormous aquarium come from post-larval captures or farms, while 100% of the coral has been grown from fragments.

WATER: THE ESSENTIAL ELEMENT

SUPPLIES ARE LIMITED!

The most vital requirement for any living organism is access to water. The paradox of these islands bathing in vast quantities of liquid, however, is that their fresh water resources are often extremely limited. This has to do with their geographical and ecological features. *Island Agenda*, a Unesco publication focusing on issues and development programmes, stresses this shortfall: "Because of their small size and particular geological, topographical and climatic conditions, many small island developing states face severe constraints in terms of both the quality and quantity of freshwater."

Low-lying coral islands are especially vulnerable, as their underground sources are, as a rule, no more than a "freshwater lens" formed by rainwater infiltration. Often covered only by a thin layer of soil, these lenses enjoy little protection against saline intrusion caused by high tides and storm waves. Seawater also slips in when drought or overuse lowers the level of these natural cisterns.

Mountainous islands, by contrast, can count on more substantial water tables, together with streams and lakes; but because their surface areas are limited, these resources, which vary according to rainfall, are not plentiful. In addition, although islands are numerous in heavy-rainfall tropical zones, lack of space means little freshwater storage potential. And on volcanic islands, the thin layer of soil covering the steep slopes can be easily washed away by violent rainstorms, with the resultant mud runoff filling any manmade reservoirs there might be. At the same time tanks and rainwater recovery techniques provide easy, inexpensive means of storing water for local communities.

And, of course, there are times of drought. On small islands water is mainly used for agricultural purposes, but tourism makes heavy demands: some island destinations have ten times more visitors annually than they have inhabitants and tourist facilities are often serviced at the expense of the locals. In addition, the variation in demand from one season to the next can complicate things even further; whence the need, for the locals, for adequate water storage, treatment and conveyancing facilities. Appropriate methods for saving water, such as the right kind of irrigation, and recycling of treated wastewater, are also indispensable.

FOLLOWING DOUBLE PAGE: THE MALDIVES ARCHIPELAGO IS MADE UP OF ALMOST 2,000 SMALL CORAL ISLANDS AND ISLETS, MOST OF THEM UNINHABITED AND SPREAD OVER A VAST MARINE TERRITORY. EVERY YEAR 200,000 TOURISTS COME TO THESE TURQUOISE WATERS FOR A TASTE OF PARADISE LOST.

CAPE VERDE: GETTING IRRIGATION RIGHT

In Cape Verde vegetable cultivation – tomatoes, onions, pepper, etc. – expanded considerably in the 1990s, but lack of water very soon proved a problem. A project organised by the United Nations Food and Agriculture Organisation (FAO) led to installation of a gravity-fed drip-irrigation system using raised tanks, which obviated the need for pumping, and this brought increased productivity together with a 40–50% saving of water. In 1999, six years after the project had begun, the system was being used on 22% of all cultivated land.[23] Many farmers have since given up growing sugar cane in favour of high-yield vegetables.

DESALINATION: BETTER METHODS NEEDED

Desalination of seawater makes fresh water possible for islands that are really in need of it. One example is Nauru, a small, extremely isolated mid-Pacific state comprising a single coral island of 21 square kilometres. Early in 2012 Nauru received funds from the Pacific Environment Community (PEC) for increasing its desalination capacity. The problem is that there are limits to desalination: it is expensive and energy-greedy, and has major environmental consequences. The use of hydrocarbons it calls for produces large quantities of greenhouse gases and so aggravates global warming. It also has radical short term impacts: if the brine – a mix of salts, minerals and chemicals – that remains after the process is dumped near the coast, it can increase sea-water salinity and damage marine ecosystems. Subsequent destruction of the coral reef and its life-cycles brings with it a loss of income for local fishermen.

This is what happened in Bahrain, a small island kingdom in the Persian Gulf whose population depends entirely on desalination for its fresh water. The country has enormous oil reserves, so the price of energy is not a problem; on the other hand, the absence of water necessitated the construction of a huge desalination plant, whose brine discharge has upset the ecological balance of the coral reef. Nonetheless, industrial experts claim that the technology is improving and that progress is being made in the processing of the waste products, which can be disposed of far from vulnerable areas. In addition, they say, the most recent plants consume less energy. In the Canary Islands studies of small solar and wind-powered desalination units have been going on for some time now, and for island states with significant renewable energy resources this could be a viable approach. Already the island of Bequia in St Vincent and the Grenadines, in the Caribbean, has its own solar-powered desalination plant.

TREATING POLLUTED WATER

Access to good-quality water is a major issue for island dwellers, yet this remains an area of inequality, since running water is often polluted by farming, industrial and domestic effluents. Largely invisible, this contamination of water not only directly affects the health of those who drink it, it also has indirect consequences in that it poisons the environment – and especially the sea.
In the often overpopulated coastal regions of developing countries, up to 90% of waste water ends up in the sea without undergoing any treatment. These effluents contain hydrocarbons, chemical pollutants, waste oil, heavy metals, and fertilisers. Often they also disperse dangerous microbes into the natural environment. All of this means that they can have a drastic impact on the natural environment, and on marine flora and fauna. In the Caribbean, for instance, where barely 20% of wastewater is treated before entering the sea, a number of bacterial and viral diseases are attacking the coral. Some of the microorganisms in question are of human origin and are killing reefs already rendered fragile by global warming. Moreover, they affect the health of bathers and by entering the food chain can contaminate consumers of fish and shellfish. This pollution, in tandem with reef degradation, has unfavourable economic fallout too, since fishing and tourism both suffer.

INTEGRATED PROJECTS IN THE CARIBBEAN

Given the nature and extent of the problem, the *Integrating Watershed and Coastal Area Management* (IWCAM) programme has been implemented in the Caribbean as a means of limiting the practice of pouring polluting effluents directly into streams and rivers. The goal, of course, is to improve the health of local communities and to preserve the environment. Several small-scale initiatives are already under way: in St Lucia, for example, there are plans for a pilot water treatment unit in the municipality of Au Léon: the system is a natural one, using an area planted with reeds and other vegetation which will filter waste water and capture the pollutants. Sustainable, ecological and inexpensive, this system is also very easy to maintain. As part of an overall strategy designed by the Caribbean Environmental Health Institute (CEHI), it is funded by the Global Environment Facility (GEF) and is coupled

with a rainwater harvesting system that will ease the water shortage problem in times of drought. The accompanying tanks will provide unpolluted water for village communities. Houses and villages equipped with collectors for this project are also given regular advice on cleaning and general upkeep. Also in St Lucia, a project in the Vieux Fort area has seen hotels saving and recycling water: consumption is said to have been reduced by 25% and the water is reused for lawns and gardens. In the wake of this experiment the government obliged all hotels to harvest rainwater and treat their wastewater.

If these individual ventures are to serve as pilot projects and be reproduced on other islands, there first has to be an experience-sharing network involving local community associations, stakeholders and institutional bodies; this would enable closer cooperation between the different parties and facilitate new projects.

ENERGY FOR SUSTAINABLE DEVELOPMENT

FAITH IN RENEWABLE ENERGY

Wood is the traditional source of energy on many islands, but has become increasingly rare with overexploitation and deforestation driven by the quest for more agricultural and urban space. Fossil fuels are frequently in short supply or non-existent: islanders have to import them, often from distant countries, which makes them even more expensive. Nonetheless, islands have a number of major assets in terms of renewable energy: not only sun, wind and sea, but also energy from the centre of the Earth.

THE SUN IS POTENTIALLY A MAJOR SOURCE OF ENERGY FOR ISLAND STATES (LEFT).
HERE, HOUSES FITTED WITH SOLAR PANELS IN GUADELOUPE, IN THE CARIBBEAN (RIGHT).

The immense potential of sun, wind and geothermal energy is sufficient to ensure island energy needs. And in addition there is now a great deal of interest in what the sea has to offer in the form of currents, waves, temperature differences between the surface and the depths, and biofuel produced from phytoplankton. In this respect islands have everything to gain: economically speaking they would cut energy costs; environmentally they would reduce greenhouse gas emissions and the risk of oil spills; and politically they would be more autonomous. Development of these new sources of energy calls for substantial material and technical input, but the important thing is that they represent a sustainable solution.

ALL THE SUN AND WIND YOU WANT

Most of the energy used on La Réunion still comes from imported coal and hydrocarbons; it was even planned at one time to build a new coal-fired power station. In addition, demand is rising along with the population and changes in lifestyle: in the last twenty years energy consumption has escalated by 350%[24]. In the housing field, for example, the traditional dwellings with their systems of natural ventilation – corridors, windows with *jalousies* – are little by little being replaced by modern, air-conditioned ones. The social unrest that sprang up on the island early in 2012 highlighted the difficulties that fuel costs are causing for a large part of the population.

While it remains highly dependent on fossil fuels – oil, coal and gas – La Réunion is working hard at developing alternative forms of energy and encouraging people to limit their electricity consumption. This island is pinning its hopes on energy autonomy and things could change radically in the years to come.

A WIND FARM IN GUADELOUPE (LEFT).
ON THE ISLAND OF NAURU, IN THE PACIFIC, THIS OBSERVATORY STUDIES THE ATMOSPHERE (RIGHT).

The Réunion Regional Council has set up its Plan for Renewable Energy and Rational Energy Use (PRERURE), a twenty-five year road map for improved energy efficiency and use of the renewable energy available on the island. In 2010 20% of La Réunion's electricity was coming from its five waterfall-driven hydroelectric plants, and ongoing development of alternative sources could reduce dependence on traditional energy even further. In 2011 the Reunion Energy Observatory (OER), a part of the Réunion Regional Energy Agency (ARER),[25] published an energy summary for the island: in 2010 renewable energy consumption increased by 5%. While fossil fuels – oil and coal – still provide 66.2% of electricity, almost 34% now comes from renewable sources – 1.3% more than in 2009. This change is mainly due to the growth of solar and wind energy: between 2009–10 solar power production rose by no less than 92%! Apartment buildings, hotels, offices and houses are increasingly equipped with solar panels and 110,289 solar water heaters were in operation late in 2010. A turn towards cooking with electricity has reduced dependence on gas and energy economy measures have reduced annual consumption growth by 3.5%. The advances in the renewable energy field have had significant social repercussions: production, installation and maintenance have generated new jobs – no small matter on an island where unemployment is running at close to 30%.

TOP: IN FIJI LOCAL CHILDREN DISCOVER THE JOYS OF SCOOTING OVER THE WAVES
IN JEAN-MICHEL COUSTEAU'S INFLATABLE DINGHY.
MIDDLE: ON THE ISLAND OF CHUMBE IN ZANZIBAR, WOMEN FOLLOW
A MARINE ENVIRONMENT AWARENESS PROGRAMME AND TRY SNORKELLING FOR THE FIRST TIME.
BOTTOM: DIVERS CHECKING THE HEALTH OF THE CORAL REEF IN TUVALU.

HARNESSING THE POWER OF THE OCEAN

La Réunion has become a focal point for experiments involving marine energy, with possibilities under study including waves, currents and temperature differences between the surface and the depths. Samples taken 1,000 metres down indicate a temperature of some 5.1°C. Brought up to the surface, this water could be used to cool the freshwater circuits of air-conditioning systems. This same temperature difference between surface and depths – 20°C as opposed to 5°C – can also be used to generate electricity. Meanwhile the energy potential of waves is being tested via the *Pelamis*, an articulated floating structure eventually intended to fuel a power station in the sea off St Pierre, in the south of the island. Another project, CETO, uses buoys set in movement by the waves and connected to turbines by a system of pumps. Other avenues currently being explored include energy generated by currents and algae, and this, like the skills and technologies already mentioned, could be reused on islands everywhere.

THE EARTH'S CORE: INEXHAUSTIBLE ENERGY

Where renewable energy is concerned, islands possess another interesting feature: many of them are situated in earthquake zones such as the Caribbean and the Ring of Fire in the Pacific. These might not be the safest places in the world, but they have enormous geothermal potential, and the heat energy rising from the Earth's core could be recovered and used to generate electricity.

To cite one example, St Lucia, in the Caribbean, is looking to use its volcanic origins to ensure energy autonomy. In technical terms it has been taking advantage of the skills of various foreign companies and is hoping to follow the example of Iceland, where a third of all electricity comes from geothermal sources and 90% of all buildings are heated by the country's countless volcanoes, fumaroles and geysers. A geothermal facility has been functioning on Guadeloupe since 1996 and other Caribbean islands are exploring the possibilities, with projects being planned or implemented in Martinique, Dominica, St Kitts and Nevis and elsewhere. Many other island states may ultimately reap the benefit of these projects, and thus find more lasting and sustainable sources of energy. By putting their faith in renewable energy they will cut both their costs and their greenhouse gas emissions, while showing continental countries the way to go.

NO OIL – BUT LOTS OF PALM TREES

Some islands have been looking into the possibility of making biofuel from – coconuts! Vanuatu, that little Pacific archipelago with only 215,000 inhabitants, is plugging coconut oil as an alternative to oil out of wells, both as fuel and for generating electricity. The Unelco-Suez company, which produces and distributes electricity for Vanuatu, has a 4-megawatt power station that burns 8,000 litres of coconut oil a week. It takes eight coconuts to produce one litre of oil. After beginning with a mix of 5% coconut oil and 95% diesel fuel, the company has now boosted the proportion to 15%. This "coco-fuel" keeps half the archipelago's inhabitants in electricity and can also be used to run diesel vehicles subject to a few minor modifications: the municipal vehicles all have "coco" engines. Cheap and relatively ecological, coco-fuel is a source of jobs while at the same time cutting down energy dependency. And the Vanuatu experiment has been taken up elsewhere: in Samoa, the Electric Power Corporation's CocoGen project is going to culminate in construction of a power station using a 30% coconut oil mix. Production of the same type of fuel is under study in the Marshall Islands, New Caledonia and elsewhere. In the Tuvalu Islands, pilot projects backed by the Alofa Tuvalu community association,[26] are investigating coconuts as an energy source, as well as production of biogas from fermenting pig slurry.

DEALING WITH REFUSE AND FIGHTING POLLUTION

DANGER, TOXIC WASTE!

With population increase and lifestyle changes, the amount of waste has considerably increased. Consumption of manufactured goods and, by extension, of the mass of detritus they give rise to, has exploded. In the poorest countries recovery and recycling remain significant activities: in Cuba and Madagascar plastic bags and bottles and spare parts from defunct appliances are eagerly reused. In some countries the inhabitants specialise, selling by weight metal and bottles collected from people's trash cans and dumps. In countries where the standard of living is slightly higher, but where the most disadvantaged cities, neighbourhoods and villages lack garbage collection infrastructures, residential zones and vacant land are littered with countless cans, plastic bags and solid rubbish. As the plastic and the chemicals that go into the manufacture of many modern technology artefacts – computers, telephones, audiovisual equipment, household appliances, batteries, cars, etc. – contain various toxic substances, these dumping grounds can damage the quality of the soil (and of anything grown in it) and water, with residents running the risk of contamination. Polluted water, too, provides a breeding ground for mosquitoes, which transmit such diseases as dengue and malaria.

In island settings the problem is even more acute than on the continents, given the lack of storage space, finance and treatment facilities. The volume of refuse can be reduced by incineration, but the process produces potentially dangerous ash and emissions. Refuse elimination is first and foremost a public health issue, but it is also an economic one, since pollution impacts on tourism. In 2004 a United Nations environment report[27] sounded the alarm with its estimate that since the early 1990s the quantity of plastic refuse in small island developing states had multiplied by 500%. This refuse is often abandoned just anywhere, sometimes ending up in the sea or mangrove swamps. The seasonal influx of tourists only exacerbates this state of affairs: they are often more numerous than the inhabitants and they generate much more refuse per head than the locals.

It is hardly surprising that the ocean is affected. Micro-refuse is sometimes ingested by turtles, birds and marine mammals, or rolls itself around them and suffocates them. Remnants of abandoned fishing nets, nylon ropes and the plastic used for holding six-packs and sealing cartons are particularly dangerous for sea-dwelling creatures.

RECYCLING: A SUSTAINABLE SOLUTION

The solution to the issue lies in working with specialist partners to limit production of refuse, finding appropriate treatment techniques and establishing markets for recycled products. Mauritius, for example, has launched awareness campaigns to control haphazard dumping, but it still remains to find ways of recycling the metal, paper, glass and plastic that are recovered. The same problem faces Barbados, in the Caribbean, where tourists are put off by the garbage in the streets and along the roadsides. Now some three quarters of the refuse produced is buried on officially designated sites and measures have been taken to recover, sort and recycle: one company collects and recycles paper and old car batteries, a second waste oil, a third plastic, glass and old tyres, and a fourth leftover metal for sorting and reselling.

Organic matter, which often represents the greater part of solid waste on small islands, can be reused: In sugar-cane producing Jamaica, 30% of agricultural waste is bagasse, the dry pulpy residue left after the extraction of juice from the cane. Whence the idea of using it to produce fuel and electricity. A bagasse power plant is already providing 5% of the national energy supply, and this is a system that could well expand in the future.

LAND AND SEA POLLUTION IS ONE OF THE MAIN SOURCES OF DEGRADATION
OF THE MARINE ENVIRONMENT, IMPACTING HEALTH, FOOD SUPPLIES AND LIVING CONDITIONS.

HERE WE SEE A DOLPHIN WHOSE FIN HAS BECOME ENTANGLED IN A SCRAP OF PLASTIC (TOP LEFT).
POLLUTING EMISSIONS A FEW METRES OFFSHORE IN THE MEDITERRANEAN (TOP RIGHT).
CORAL KILLED BY POLLUTION-INDUCED BLEACHING (BOTTOM LEFT).
CHILDREN ON AN UNAUTHORIZED GARBAGE DUMP IN MADAGASCAR (BOTTOM RIGHT).

THILAFUSHI IN THE MALDIVES HAS BEEN NICKNAMED TRASHCAN ISLAND. THIS IS WHERE THE CAPITAL'S REFUSE IS DUMPED, WITH PART OF THE ISLAND RENTED OUT TO SHIPBUILDING, CEMENT-MANUFACTURING AND OTHER CONCERNS

THE MALDIVES: THE END OF TRASHCAN ISLAND?

The Maldives archipelago is home to 270,000 people and welcomes 650,000 tourists every year. The artificial island of Thilafushi, created by filling in a shallow lagoon not far from Malé, the capital, has been used as a garbage dump since 1992. For the first few years the garbage was buried under sand, and parts of the island were rented out for industrial activities like boat-building. But Thilafushi, originally 7 kilometres long by 200 metres wide, soon became too small for the 300 metric tons of refuse delivered daily by barge, and now the heaps of garbage spill over into the sea, with the island's area increasing by 1 cubic metre every day. What has become known as "trash-can island" has no infrastructures for receiving and treating these mounting quantities of garbage: different areas have been designated for metal, glass, plastic and so on, but the Bangladeshi workers whose job it is to burn the refuse also throw part of it into the sea, where it builds up. Heavy metals like lead and mercury are left lying on the ground, and if they made their way into the sea, they could cause serious pollution. The high walls surrounding the dump are not enough to prevent leakages of toxic substances.

In an attempt to resolve the problem, the Maldives are now exporting metal, cans and cartons to India for recycling; this both reduces the local quantity of refuse and brings in foreign currency, but is insufficient on its own. The government has stated its intention of organising better refuse management, and technical assistance partnerships with foreign countries are envisaged. Late in 2011 the lagoon was cleaned up and dumping was restricted; these are preliminaries to more stringent regulations, which include hotels being urged to install incinerators and set up sorting, compaction and recycling systems.

A YEARNING FOR ISLANDS: IS TOURISM AN ANSWER?

MORE AND MORE VISITORS

Seaside tourism looms large in all countries with their own coastline. In worldwide terms tourism has been growing steadily for decades now: 25 million international tourists in 1950, 277 million in 1980, 684 million in 2000 and 922 million in 2008. According to the World Tourist Organization (UNWTO), the economic slump caused a 4% drop – to only 880 million – but the figure is already tending to rise again.[28] With destinations diversifying, tourism is now one of the main sources of revenue for many developing countries, as well as a crucial factor in development and job-creation. In island states the number of tourists showed a steady 10% annual growth rate between 1986 and 2004, and the number of jobs it generated almost doubled over the same period: these include direct employment in the industry and indirect jobs in the sectors providing tourist products and services. But if tourism is to be a real factor for sustainable development, it must not harm the environment and must contribute to improved living conditions for local people.

Dealing with the seasonal influx of tourists is a real challenge, especially when their numbers exceed those of full-time residents. In 2003 the Cook Islands, with a population of 20,000, took in almost 78,000 international tourists. The Bahamas, in the Caribbean, had 1,510,000 visitors (the population is 312,000) and 278,000 tourists discovered the British Virgin Islands, home to only 12,600 residents.[29] In this kind of situation requirements in terms of food, water and energy rise steeply, especially as foreigners tend to consume much more than the locals. Further consequences are an increase in imported goods and, particularly, in the quantity of wastewater to be collected and treated. Pressure on the natural setting multiplies with use, and water sports especially – swimming, sailing, diving, recreational fishing – can damage beaches and reefs and interfere with the reproductive cycles of marine birds, reptiles and fauna.

BUILDING TOURIST FACILITIES ON THE SEA

Islands wanting to cultivate tourism must have the necessary infrastructures, and these take up space. In order not to impinge on their valuable forests and farmland, some island countries have had no qualms about building on the sea: accommodation, port facilities and landing strips. Constructed entirely out of coral limestone, the artificial paradise of Eden Island, just off the coast of Mahé in the Seychelles, is covered with mansions for sale to wealthy foreigners, who anchor their sailing yachts in the marina there.

This type of project means that certain areas can be devoted to tourist activity – and thus bring in foreign currency – without encroaching on limited local space. The revenue this tourism has brought to the Seychelles is pumped back into nature preservation. However, the construction of artificial islands poses certain problems: use of coral, filling-in of the littoral and exploitation of sand and gravel from fragile coastal areas all have consequences for the marine context. In many cases erosion increases, reefs are damaged or stifled by sediment and pollution gets worse. On a large scale, then, this cannot be seen as a truly sustainable solution.

THE ENVIRONMENT AS SURETY FOR RESPONSIBLE TOURISM

Tourism affects many different sectors of island life, and all sorts of attempts have been made to reconcile economic development with respect for local culture and preservation of the environment. Tourism really can help to improve quality of life for island communities if it is accompanied by appropriate distribution of the wealth it generates: new jobs and investment of profits in the local economy. When visitors consume local resources they help the domestic market – industry and services – to develop. Hotels and restaurants where the emphasis is on local products offer outlets for farming and fishing. Tourism can also encourage local crafts and cultural events – festivals, music, art exhibitions – without necessarily lapsing into fake folklore or exploitation. This is a sector that represents a real opportunity for islanders, but it calls for substantial investment not only of money, but also of skills, management and supervision.

Furthermore, tourist activity must take account of preservation of the environment if nature is to continue to provide the ecological goods and services all people need. Protection of natural sites is vital to promotion of tourism, since beauty and diversity determine the appeal of a given destination. Every year more and more people are drawn to these ocean lands by dreams of pristine, virgin islands.

The economic input of tourism is a powerful incentive for protection of wild fauna and flora. Nowadays more and more marine protected areas and nature reserves are being created with a view to preserving the most valuable forests, mountain regions and wetlands. Every year, hiking, diving and generally getting acquainted with nature draw more tourists, and island dwellers have realised that activities like these call for sustainable management. Large numbers of divers, for example, can damage reefs by breaking off fragile coral branches and disturbing or driving away fish and marine mammals. This means it is particularly important that diving groups should be accompanied by well-trained guides. Other tactics involve restricting the number of people on any diving site at any one time, and the introduction of special management taxes.

Restricting visitor numbers is vital to ensuring that tourism observes sustainable development criteria. As Claude Colin, former attaché at the French Embassy in the Seychelles, has remarked, "Tourism is continuing to expand. Right now we have 170,000 visitors per year, but the current plan envisages a total of 230,000: this is the maximum compatible with maintaining a high standard in the Seychelles with regard to accommodation infrastructures and the water supply."

While mass tourism – gigantic hotels, beaches reserved for tourists and cut off from local life – is a fact of life in many places, projects meeting sustainable development criteria are currently under way in the Solomons, Dominican Republic, Micronesia, the Bahamas, the Seychelles, the Maldives, the Caribbean and elsewhere. In some cases these involve small organisations offering the visitor a protected natural setting. Often

EDEN ISLAND IN SEYCHELLES IS AN ARTIFICIAL MARINA LINKED TO THE ISLAND OF MAHÉ BY A BRIDGE.
ITS LUXURY RESIDENCES ARE SOLD TO RICH FOREIGNERS.

DE POSIDONIES
Labre Vert
Saupe
Nacre

this is a matter of high-end tourism, with the restrictions on numbers being compensated for by high prices, but this kind of initiative is becoming more and more accessible as new tourism models take shape. Many organisations now stress a responsible tourism that contributes positively to local development. An exhaustive list is not possible here, but interestingly inventive approaches are being tried out by the Megaptera Association in Mayotte and at Chumbe Island Coral Park in Zanzibar.

Founded in 1998 by Michel Vely, a French veterinarian in Mayotte, Megaptera has since organised numerous studies and awareness and conservation campaigns revolving around marine mammals, dugongs and whale sharks in Mayotte, the small island of St Marie, off Madagascar, and the Comoros. An "ecovoluntary" association, Megaptera offers whale experts observation trips in return for partial coverage of costs: participants pay for the ocean voyage, but their accommodation and meals are provided free by partner tour operators and hotels. On board they act as guides and lecturers for the paying public and also take part in Megaptera's scientific monitoring programme. In addition the association trains local guides in Madagascar. This system works well for all concerned: it heightens the awareness of foreign tourists and local tourism personnel, contributes to the preservation of marine mammals and other endangered species, and promotes a responsible attitude to island tourism in mainland countries.

In Zanzibar, the small, long-uninhabited island of Chumbe, 8 kilometres southwest of Stone Town, is home to a preservation project financed by ecotourism. Chumbe Island Coral Park is a marine protected area created and run by a private company: here visitors can discover both virgin forest and a pristine coral reef. "Local fishermen have been given new jobs managing natural resources," explains park director Sibylle Riedmiller. "They work as guides, take part in scientific work, head up education programmes and supervise diving. Lots of students and people from local NGOs come to Chumbe Island Coral Park for a hands-on introduction to sustainable development." Some 35% of the tourism revenue goes towards park management, which includes educational projects for children and teachers in addition to the monitoring and research carried out by the personnel. The seven ecobungalows on the island have been designed to minimise environmental impact and feature solar energy, compost toilets, rainwater harvesting and natural filtration of wastewater. "This is a private venture," Sibylle Riedmiller continues, "but it is non-profit. In 2011, in the United Nations Secretary General's preliminary report for Rio+20,[30] Chumbe Island Coral Park was cited as a showcase for sustainable financing of protected areas." The park has received many ecotourism awards and in 2000 was nominated by the United Nations Environment Programme (UNEP) for outstanding environmental achievement.

THE FIRST OR SECOND ECONOMIC SECTOR FOR MANY ISLANDS, TOURISM CAN BE GIVEN A CONSERVATION SLANT, AS IN THIS UNDERWATER DISCOVERY TRAIL IN THE PORT-CROS MARINE PARK IN THE MEDITERRANEAN (TOP). A SCHOOL OF FISH UNDER A CABIN ON STILTS IN A POLYNESIAN LAGOON (BOTTOM).

JEAN-MICHEL COUSTEAU COMMITS TO ECOTOURISM IN FIJI

Fiji: this Pacific Ocean country of 800,000 inhabitants comprises 322 islands and 522 islets, representing a little more than 18,000 square kilometres. The two biggest islands – Viti Levu and Vanua Levu – are covered with tropical forest and have mountain peaks rising to 1,300 metres. The ancestors of Polynesia's people arrived here around 1240 BCE, followed later by other populations of Melanesian origin. Europeans took up residence in the nineteenth century, with British control leading to the immigration of a large Indian community. Three quarters of the population live on Viti Levu and the official languages are Fijian, English and Hindustani. Tourism is a major economic resource, with some 300 to 400,000 visitors annually. Pilot tourist facilities based on sustainable development criteria have been tried out on different scales: small, community association ventures offering eco-volunteer programmes; island-hopping introductions to the natural environment; and hotels with ecological water, energy and refuse recycling facilities. In Vanua Levu's Savusavu Bay, Jean-Michel Cousteau – son of the famed Jacques Cousteau – is partner in a hotel venture founded entirely on ecological criteria. Richard Murphy, scientific director of Ocean Futures Society, founded by Jean-Michel Cousteau, tells how the project began: "In 1995 Jean-Michel Cousteau and his team had the opportunity to convert a hotel in Fiji into a model sustainable development tourist infrastructure. Drawing on the functioning of a coral reef, we came up with a concept that takes advantage of the ecological services nature offers free of charge, the idea being to minimise environmental impact and cut costs. We use integrated systems including waste water treatment and recycling, organic pest control, restoration of mangrove forests to prevent coastal erosion and preservation of the natural vegetation to provide a habitat for birds." Everything, then, is designed to minimise pollution and environmental impact. Refuse is recycled and the wastewater filtration system uses coconuts and recycled plastic bottles which gradually become coated with an anti-bacterial film. After filtration the water is conveyed to an ecological treatment plant – a generously planted wetland area – and is then used for watering. Organic waste is turned into compost for the garden, which supplies vegetables for the hotel's restaurant. Energy is hydraulic. Visitors to Fiji Island Cousteau Resort have the chance to take part in discovery activities such as exploring the mangrove swamps and diving in the Koro Sea. The hotel's full-time salaried biologist monitors the biodiversity situation, with one venture being reintroduction of the giant clam into the bay. He also supervises ongoing studies of the reef and passes the results on to the international body Reef Check.[31] Encounters and interchange between visitors and locals are another feature.

"Our mix of economic efficiency and ecological know-how means we can offer guests an intellectually, spiritually and physically enriching setting," explains Richard Murphy. "It is a source of inspiration for people seeking to combine quality of life with greater sustainability. In the 1990s this approach was far from common and the success of our project has helped promote sound practices in environmentally conscious tourist ventures."

Islands in a Warmer World

For some years now the little atoll of Takuu, in Papua New Guinea, has been hit by increasingly frequent king tides that flood the village, its taro fields and its burial grounds; and the inhabitants may soon have to move to less exposed islands nearby. Global warming is the major disruption islands currently have to cope with. Its consequences are many and represent a real threat to the survival of island populations now engaged in a day-to-day struggle to preserve their land, water resources, fields and homes.

UPHEAVAL ON A GLOBAL SCALE

The extent of today's climate change is linked to an increase in the greenhouse effect. By favouring heat absorption, water vapour, carbon dioxide, methane and nitrogen protoxide play their part in the natural greenhouse effect, but increased emissions of these gases due to human activity has led to a rapid, substantial alteration of the Earth's climate. Already the worldwide upheaval triggered by climate change is having visible effects: the atmosphere, the ocean and the soil are affected, and the water cycle, polar regions, forests, glaciers, winds and deserts are changing before our very eyes. The scientists who share their findings via the Intergovernmental Panel on Climate Change (IPCC) are producing models they hope will help with prediction of climate change effects. This is an immense, complex task, with the many factors involved interacting with each other over a vast area. Prediction is made even more complicated by the fact that the effects of global warming vary from one part of the world to another. What we do know, however, is that these effects include rises in sea level, changes in ocean circulation patterns, melting of glaciers and the polar ice caps, and changes in wind and storm patterns; together with increased rain and flooding in some areas and drought and fires in others. The increase of carbon dioxide will also result in ocean acidification. All living creatures are going to feel the impact of this environmental turmoil: some will adapt and others will move elsewhere, but those unable to do either face extinction. Marine and land biodiversity is going to change: death of coral, an exodus of fish and marine invertebrates, disappearance of land-based plant and animal species, invasions of species from warmer zones, proliferation of certain micro-organisms, etc. And this in turn means changes in the natural resources humanity depends on for its survival.

PREVIOUS DOUBLE PAGE: ON TUVALU, IN THE PACIFIC, INCREASINGLY FREQUENT GIANT TIDES SUBMERGE COASTAL ROADS AND OTHER FACILITIES.

A RESIDENT OF TUVALU, AMONG THE COUNTRIES MOST THREATENED BY RISING SEA LEVELS.

According to the experts the rise in sea level, which was 15 to 17 centimetres in the course of the twentieth century, is going to reach 20 to 60 centimetres by the end of the twenty-first. And this estimate could be too low, given the inadequacy of present efforts to reduce greenhouse gas emissions. The rise in the sea level reflects a combination of two factors: the melting of glaciers and polar ice due to increasing atmospheric temperatures; and ocean water dilation. The consequences for islands, as land masses surrounded by the ocean, are already drastic.

ISLANDS IN THE FRONT LINE

On 12 February 2012 Nauruan ambassador Marlene Moses made it clear in her inaugural speech as president of the Alliance of Small Island States (AOSIS), that climate change is the big issue for islands: "We know that the international response to the climate crisis falls well short of what is needed, not just to protect island people, but all of the world's inhabitants. To that end, we are looking at ways to ratchet up emissions reduction ambition and to partner with committed countries to find the additional reductions that science shows are needed to give all of our members a fighting chance for survival."

It is not easy to predict with any certainty the situation island dwellers will have to cope with in ten, twenty or thirty years, but they have already been witnessing modification of their environment for some time. With the rise in average sea levels king tides are more frequent, and when the sea sweeps over shoreline areas it both encroaches on an island's freshwater reserves and leaves behind salt which damages crops and the soil. Many Pacific atolls have seen their coconut palms decimated and their coastlines increasingly eroded by wave action. It is estimated that coral reefs, because they form a natural barrier, reduce erosion by absorbing 70 to 90% of the impact of waves; but these reefs are deteriorating as water temperatures rise: above 30°C, 1 or 2 degrees more are enough to make the coral expel the *zooxanthellae*, the symbiotic algae that live inside them, and when this happens the coral bleaches and ultimately dies. This phenomenon varies according to coral species and locations: Red Sea coral, for example, are more used to temperature changes and so are less affected, whereas in Malaysia, where temperatures are very constant, coral is highly sensitive. Whitening or bleaching of coral reefs is sometimes due to natural causes: El Niño, a cyclical climate pattern occurring across the tropical Pacific Ocean roughly every five years, alters marine currents and triggers major disruptions of the ocean's ecosystem, but its frequency is now being accentuated by climate change. Pollution can also cause the death of coral, as can degradation of a reef caused by buildings on the shore and insensitive coastline development. And when the coral dies, tropical islands' resistance to climate change diminishes. A vicious circle.

SALINISATION PRODUCED BY RISING SEA LEVELS IS CUTTING BACK AVAILABLE FARMLAND AND DEGRADING THE SOIL AT THE SAME TIME.
HERE, AN ISLET IN THE BAHAMAS AND A BEACH IN POLYNESIA (FACING PAGE).

WEATHERING THE STORM

The warming process we are now witnessing has another consequence: the weather has gone haywire. Longer than average periods of drought strike some regions while torrential rain batters others, exacerbating an already fragile water balance. The general rise in atmospheric temperatures may accentuate the already considerable pressure on freshwater reserves: crops require more water if harvests are not to decline. The surface of the sea is becoming warmer, giving rise to the abnormal increase in evaporation that is the cause of big tropical storms. According to some experts we are in for a marked increase in violent cyclones, hurricanes and typhoons.

Despite enormous efforts by scientists, the future remains extremely uncertain. Not all the possible natural disasters are going to happen, and some effects may even prove locally beneficial: increased rainfall, for example. But the stakes are such that we can readily understand that no country in the world wants to endure the full effects of global warming – which, however things turn out, is going to mean profound change for those living in the most exposed areas. Coastal erosion, soil loss, salinization of soil and freshwater sources, the death of coral reefs: these are already a reality for many island dwellers.

OUTPOSTS FOR CLIMATE STUDY

In Nauru, a small island state in the Pacific, meteorology staff from the Ministry of Development and Industry carry out daily checks of clouds, temperatures and sunlight intensity. Given their front line position with regard to climate change, islands generally are especially important research venues. The ARM Climate Research Facility[32] is an American institution for the study of changes in the climate, and manages a number of observation stations in strategic spots including the Maldives, Nauru and Manus in Papua New Guinea. These observatories function in partnership with governmental and scientific bodies in the host countries, with ARM focusing in particular on clouds and the role of aerosols. Says information officer Lynne Roeder, "Our aim is to describe the atmosphere so as to resolve uncertainties in our climate models and come up with sustainable solutions to the energy and environmental challenges facing the United States. The tropical region of the West Pacific plays an important part in the annual variability of the Earth's climate. Data collected on small islands are much scarcer than measurements from the continents, but they are vital to a realistic picture of the tendencies and climate systems of tomorrow."

In Hawaii carbon dioxide levels in the air have been measured month by month since 1950 by scientists from the Mauna Loa observatory, responsible to the National Oceanic and Atmospheric Administration (NOAA), the American agency in charge of ocean and atmosphere studies.[33] Mauna Loa is the perfect spot: its isolated setting means it is hardly affected by the presence of vegetation or human activity. A second NOAA observatory in American Samoa also affects regular checks of the gas composition of the atmosphere.

Analysis of results is a fundamental part of establishing models and predictions governments can draw on in shaping their responses to global warming. "Computer models," Lynne Roeder goes on, "are the only tool researchers have for simulating climate change to come. The accuracy of these models depends on in-the-field observation, such as the data collected by ARM. When the authorities have a clearer idea of climate variations, it's easier for them to take decisions relating to energy and technology policy and strategies for reducing greenhouse gases. And since the climate affects everybody, it's also important to have a public that's aware of the connections between the various climate systems and of what scientists are doing to improve prediction tools."

LOOKING ANXIOUSLY TO THE FUTURE

For several years now the media have been stressing the threat represented by the rising level of the world's oceans. In tropical zones countries made up mainly of coral atolls are anxious at the prospect of being submerged only decades from now: most of them are only a few metres above sea level, and given their limited size they have no real inland areas to fall back on. As huge tides become more and more common, coastal erosion continues, so that the biggest islands are watching their area diminish as their population increases. The smallest islands are quite simply afraid of disappearing; among the most threatened are the Maldives, Kiribatis, Tuvalu, Marshalls, others off the coast of Papua New Guinea, Tokelau and a host of Polynesian atolls. Faced with the alarming news coming in from scientists, governments and community associations, the inhabitants of these island states are very worried people, and there is even talk of displacing communities living on the most endangered islands. In 2006 Susie Saitala Kofe, a Tuvalu jurist and president of the Alofa Tuvalu (Love Tuvalu) association,[34] wondered, "If that were really to happen, and we had to be moved to another country, what would we call ourselves?" With a population of 10,000, Tuvalu comprises nine islands – six of them atolls – with a total area of 26 square kilometres and the highest point 4.5 metres above sea level (the average

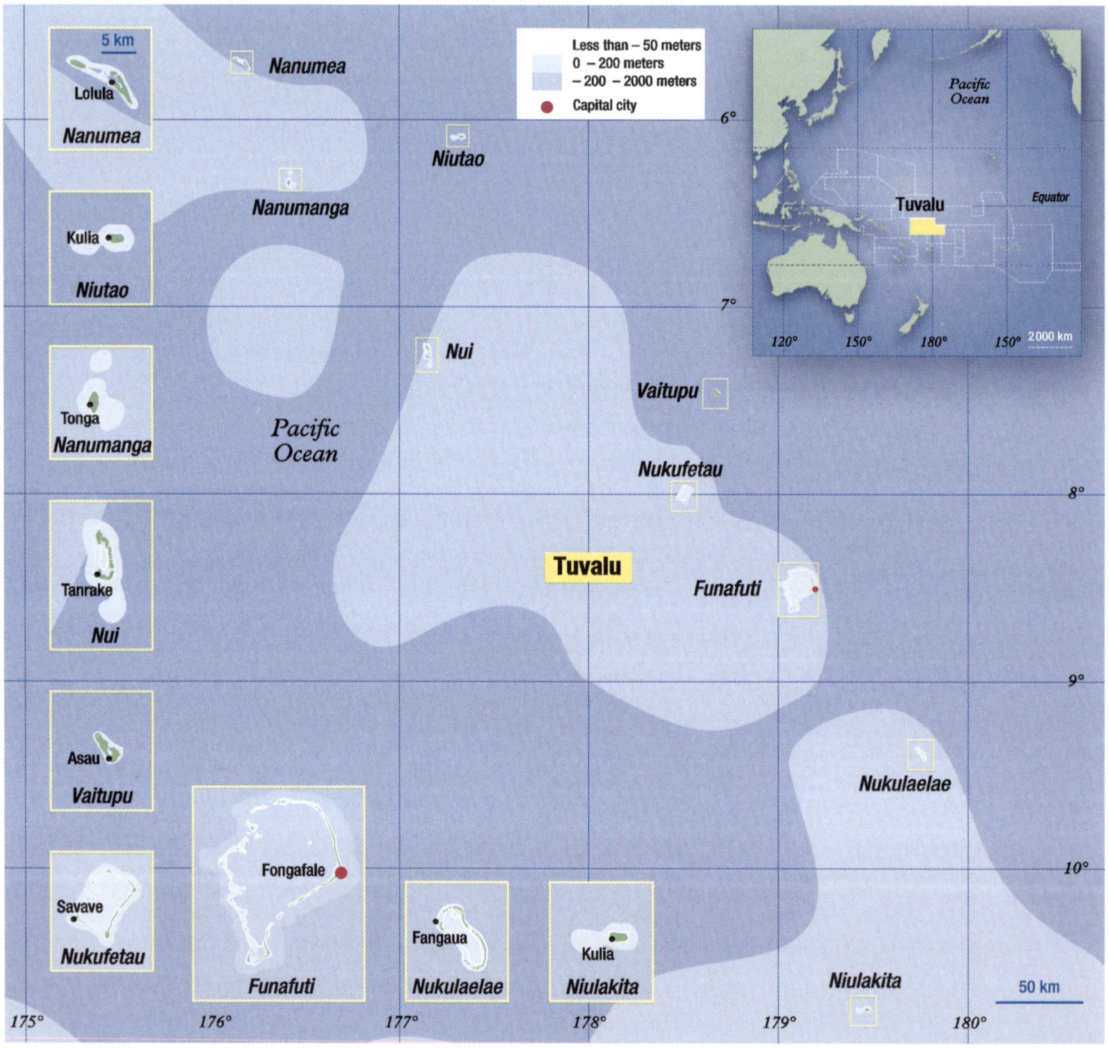

THE REPUBLIC OF TUVALU IN THE PACIFIC HAS SOME 10,500 INHABITANTS LIVING ON ITS NINE CORAL ATOLLS.

altitude being 1.5 metres). In February 2004 the islands were battered by waves 3 metres high, and according to local weather reports they have been regularly flooded since 2000 by seawater coming up through the ground. Initially coinciding with the big spring tides, this is now happening almost every month, with the added salt degrading the islands' soil and already limited freshwater stocks. Some experts say the country will be uninhabitable by 2050. There is now an emigration agreement with New Zealand, already home to some 3,000 Tuvaluans, allowing the entry of 75 extra workers per year: a certain number of the local people are ready to emigrate to find work, and the overseas community is doing its best to maintain its culture and identity. With a view to ensuring the country's survival, Alofa Tuvalu has launched a "Small is Beautiful" plan emphasising an exemplary approach to environmental matters. The plan includes implementation of concrete, reproducible measures for reduction of greenhouse gas emissions and their promotion all over the world as part of the fight against global climate change. In the spring of 2012 the association published a position paper drawing up an inventory of local marine biodiversity, itself much affected by climatic disturbances.

FUNAFUTI, TUVALU'S MAIN ISLAND, IS A NARROW STRIP OF LAND 2.8 SQUARE KILOMETRES IN AREA AND WITH ITS HIGHEST POINT ONLY A FEW METRES ABOVE SEA LEVEL.

FOLLOWING DOUBLE PAGE: MANY SEA-FRONT TOURIST FACILITIES, AS HERE IN POLYNESIA, WILL BE SERIOUSLY AFFECTED BY RISING SEA LEVELS; AND TOURISM IS A KEY SECTOR OF THE ISLAND'S ECONOMY.

Tuvalu Overview, another association founded by Japanese photographer Shuichi Endo,[35] has set out to alert a wider public to the situation and to find solutions to global warming problems. Its project "Build the Future with 10,000 Tuvaluans"[36] involves collecting photos of every inhabitant, together with their accounts of life there, thus giving them the chance to communicate with the rest of the world via the project's Internet site. Already 2,400 residents from four of the islands have been interviewed by the Tuvalu Overview team: when questioned in January to March 2012, 98% of the 803 inhabitants of Vaitupu declared they loved being where they are. So maybe a lifestyle based on close ties with nature and free of any urge to accumulate wealth is an ingredient for a happy life. The association has also set up ventures including water management and mangrove replanting as a counter to coastal erosion.

TAKUU: LIVING ON BORROWED TIME?

400 people live on Takuu atoll, 250 kilometres northeast of Bougainville in Papua New Guinea. For several years now the island has been a regular victim of king tides that sweep into the village and the gardens where the islanders cultivate taro. In 2008 the village was flooded three times in three days.[37] Protective walls have been built along the shore, but the waves tend to undermine them and the erosion process seems even worse than before. Even if the island does not vanish beneath the surface very soon, living conditions are becoming steadily more difficult. What can be done to ensure a future for the community? The government has found a possible site on the island of Bougainville, but few of the residents want to leave: the thought of being separated from their land, their religious sites and their houses is heartbreaking, and they fear that living far from home they will be unable to preserve their language and culture.

CLIMATE CHANGE: AN ECONOMIC AND SOCIAL PREDICAMENT

For island peoples the most feared consequences of global warming naturally have to do with safety: their physical safety, especially in the event of cyclones, tidal waves and flooding. But there are other problems too, with the potential for ruinous economic and social impact: health problems, for example, triggered by the declining quality and quantity of drinking water; and the fact that increased rainfall can lead to the proliferation of insects carrying infectious diseases. Food supplies are threatened, and jobs in the agricultural sector, especially on the atolls, are endangered by drought, salinisation and erosion. Farmers may find themselves forced to work in entirely different ways.

Already fishermen are having to adapt to changes in marine biodiversity, and are fishing elsewhere or concentrating on different species. Environmental change demands changes in habits and a search for new resources and new ways of living; and all these transitions require time, adaptability and imagination. In the most economically fragile countries cooperation and pooling of resources between states, together with international solidarity and exchanges of experiences, are essential to limiting the social and economic repercussions of global warming.

CUSHIONING CHANGE AND LEARNING TO ADAPT

THE KIRIBATIS TAKE A STAND

Year after year, and from one summit meeting to the next, Republic of Kiribati president Anote Tong travels the world calling attention to his country's plight. There, greenhouse gas emissions are among the world's lowest: per head, some 2% of what an American produces. But while the 100,000 inhabitants of this small Pacific archipelago are in no way responsible for today's global upheavals, their everyday life has altered radically.

The problems are climate change and rising sea levels. The vast majority of the islands are no more than a few hundred metres across at their widest points and their maximum altitude is 3 metres, with the sole exception of Banaba, which rises to 80 metres. Being so narrow, the islands offer no refuge when things go wrong, and for the last few years the height and frequency of the waves has been steadily increasing. Waves of up to 2.8 metres are now a fact of life, sweeping the islands from end to end, as violent storms also become more regular occurrences. The government, however, is not taking things lying down, and its plan for coping with the effects of climate change has three main emphases: combating flooding, protection

of freshwater resources, and public awareness. Water management and rainwater harvesting have been improved; walls have been built along the most exposed sections of the shoreline; and replanting of mangroves is being used to protect the coast. Studies are also being made of ways to make public infrastructures – the roads, the airport – more resistant to damage by the sea, while coastline development is designed to minimise the danger to the inhabitants and cut back erosion. Currently development funding from Australia, New Zealand, Japan and the European Union is being used to finance water management programmes and work on renewable forms of energy. Will this ambitious plan succeed in making the country habitable in the long term? Given the looming difficulties, all the angles are being covered, with one of the options being emigration of the population to neighbouring Pacific countries. In February 2012 Anote Tong went to Fiji to see about buying land there for the I-Kiribati, as the inhabitants are called. Six months earlier, at the 2011 Pacific Islands Forum in New Zealand, he did not exclude the possibility of creating floating artificial islands, like giant oil rigs. Estimated cost of the operation: 2 billion dollars.

In other words, the price to be paid for adapting to climate change could be very high indeed, especially for island nations who do not consider themselves responsible for the situation and whose economies are not strong enough to offer their populations the necessary protective measures. And so they are appealing to the international community, as Anote Tong did at the Copenhagen Climate Summit in 2009: "We are a proud people. We do not come to Copenhagen as beggars – that is not our way. But we cannot face this huge challenge without international support – both practical and moral. [...] To turn your back and watch your neighbour go down when you could have done something – I think that's immoral, and

WHEN THE WATER TEMPERATURE RISES, CORALS BLEACH AND DIE, AND THE REEF IS DEGRADED.
AT PRESENT SOME TWO-THIRDS OF THE WORLD'S REEFS ARE CONSIDERED UNDER THREAT.

calls into question our humanity, and the way we treat each other as members of the human family."

A NATIONAL ACTION PLAN IN THE MALDIVES

Situated 450 kilometres south of India, the 1,200 islands of the Maldives archipelago are a little taste of Paradise in the middle of the Indian Ocean. And yet this country of 310,000 people has many urgent problems on its hands – and the impact of global warming is not the least of them. It is in much the same predicament as the Kiribatis, with a maximum altitude of 2 metres and 80% of its territory only a single metre above sea level. To alert international opinion to its perilous state, in 2009 the Council of Ministers met around a table six metres below the surface. Wearing wetsuits and equipped with scuba gear, the then president Mohamed Nasheed and ten ministers signed a resolution calling for worldwide reduction of carbon dioxide emissions, and committed the country to "Zero Carbon" by 2020.

At the same time the Maldives are not sitting back waiting for the big, most polluting countries to commit more actively to countering greenhouse gases. For several decades now they have been working at ways of protecting their scattered territories against the assaults of the ocean. Since the late 1980s North Malé Atoll, home to the capital, Malé, has been ringed with breakwaters and concrete dykes. Overpopulated and totally urbanised, the capital has no room left for expansion: already two raised artificial islands have been constructed on the coral reef 2 kilometres away, one to accommodate a part of the population, and the other to provide

AS ON MANY CORAL ISLANDS, BLOCKS OF CORAL ARE A BASIC BUILDING MATERIAL (LEFT).
A SCIENTIST FROM THE AMERICAN-ORGANISED ATMOSPHERIC RADIATION MEASUREMENT (ARM) TAKES MEASUREMENTS ON THE ISLAND OF GAN IN THE MALDIVES (RIGHT).

room for an international airport. Work on the first island, Hulhumalé, began in 1997, when the lagoon was filled in with millions of tons of sand and dead coral. Now apartment blocks, a hospital, a school and a mosque occupy an area 1.7 kilometres long, 400 metres wide and 2 metres above sea level. Not far away, on the second artificial island of Hulhulé, is the airport, linked to the capital by a ferry. A different solution has been adopted for the rest of the archipelago, where the scattered atoll communities are being regrouped on the biggest, highest islands. The Maldives bore the full brunt of the 2004 tsunami (see page 69) and since then anxiety about the danger from the sea has made Maldivians more accepting of the need to move. Information campaigns aimed at schools and the general public have also increased awareness of the crucial environmental issues the country has to face. And funding for the various measures now comes in part from a special tourist tax. Concrete alone will not solve the problem of rising sea levels. In addition to being very costly, construction of breakwaters and dykes creates its own dilemma in that it undermines the health of the beaches: normally – but not any more – the sand is moved about by the currents and comes to rest naturally on the shore. So it is now particularly important that the natural defences of the coral islands should be preserved and even restored. The Maldives' reefs are home to 250 kinds of coral and over 1,000 species of fish, and are vitally important in terms not only of the revenue generated by fishing and tourism, but also of the protection from the sea they provide. Many of them have been damaged, especially by the taking of coral for use as a building material; and in the late 1990s an outbreak of bleaching killed as much as 90% of the coral in some areas. As a result the government has taken preventive measures: it is now forbidden to remove even dead coral and protected areas have been created, among them Baa, one of Republic of Maldives' 26 geographical atolls, which was declared a Unesco World Biosphere Reserve in 2011. This decision followed in the wake of a new popular awareness of the vital role natural settings play in everyone's survival. A recent study indicated that some 89% of the Maldives' gross domestic product depends on biodiversity.[38] The country is now hoping that this improved public image will bring in more tourist dollars, but a handsome reef in good health requires more than just preservation: there has to be restoration as well, and for this "coral farms" have been set up (see box, page 198).

MANGROVE FORESTS AND COASTAL BUFFERING

Another vital contributor to island survival is the mangrove swamp, a coastal forest of trees able to flourish in seawater. Mangroves grow naturally throughout the tropical belt, in mud flats or shoreline areas with only a very slight slope. The intricately

ESPECIALLY THREATENED BY CLIMATE CHANGE, ISLAND STATES ARE STRIVING TO ALERT THE INTERNATIONAL COMMUNITY TO THE NEED TO CUT BACK GREENHOUSE GAS EMISSIONS: HERE, AN ATOLL IN THE MALDIVES.

FOLLOWING DOUBLE PAGE: THE MANGROVES THAT GROW IN SEAWATER ALONG TROPICAL COASTS ALSO SERVE AS BREEDING GROUNDS: AMONG THEIR ROOTS LARVAE AND YOUNG MARINE CREATURES ARE SAFE FROM PREDATORS.

REEFS: NATURAL RAMPARTS AGAINST THE OCEAN

In 2001, the environmental consultancy Seamarc, directed by Thomas Le Berre, a Frenchman who has been living in the Maldives for almost fifteen years, formed a partnership with the Four Seasons Resort hotel complex in Baa, to finance a "coral cuttings" programme titled "Reefscapers": "It was pretty much by chance that I got involved," explains Le Berre. "After opting for the Maldives as home, I set about doing what I knew how to do: coastal oceanography. In particular I worked on beach maintenance techniques, and this got me interested in the origin of sediments and the natural defences whose "building blocks" were coral. That's when the director of the Four Seasons Resort asked me to take over the reef restoration project he had started, but was having trouble with. I worked on it for several years with strictly relative results, then I changed over to the 'coral structures' method we're still using and improving now."

The method involves taking pieces of coral, breaking them up into "cuttings" and mounting them on a metal frame – the structure – that is then submerged in the sea. The coral regenerates and grows and a new colony takes shape. "There are two standard approaches to coastal protection," Le Berre continues. "The first is 'heavy engineering', which completely replaces the reef's protective function with a wall of concrete. This is effective but costly, and often pays no heed to biodiversity and the natural beauty of the marine landscape. The second method consists in preserving the natural defences by protection and regulation. Our 'alternative engineering' approach is somewhere between the two: we try to encourage the natural functions which, in this particular case, are endangered by global climate change."

By 2011 over 2,000 coral-producing structures were in place – a total of 160,000 transplanted cuttings – and now a new reef is being born. The surrounds also benefit from the programme, since at reproduction time the coral lays eggs, which are dispersed by the currents and repopulate the neighbouring area. Local communities are part of the project, notably for making the frames for the cuttings. With a view to extending its activities Reefscapers also offers the public the chance to sponsor a coral structure, which is then named after the donor, who receives regular information and photos of the progress of "his" or "her" reef. "This is a very general kind of technique," stresses Thomas Le Berre, "and it could easily be used elsewhere. It's very likely that the 'heavy engineering' method will provide more 'practical' solutions, either as fill for reclamation purposes and making artificial islands, or for protecting economically vital infrastructures such as harbours, airports, etc. It's also more than possible that a few decades from now coral reefs will

TOP: PROTECTION OF CORAL REEFS IS NOW A PRIORITY FOR MOST TROPICAL ISLAND STATES AND SCIENTIFIC MONITORING IS THE WATCHWORD, AS HERE IN POLYNESIA.
BOTTOM: IN THE MALDIVES CORAL "CUTTINGS" ARE SET INTO METAL STRUCTURES AS A WAY OF CREATING NEW CORAL REEFS.

be relegated to natural history museums and public aquariums. It might sound pessimistic, but in spite of the progress we've made, there's still an awful lot to do. Then again, only ten years ago large-scale coral propagation seemed impossible; so we still have enough time left to understand these ecosystems and save them." No question, technical advances in reef restoration are coming thick and fast and spreading all over the world; but initiatives like the one in the Maldives need to be greatly expanded if we are to halt the disturbing disappearance of our coral.

meshed roots keep sediment in place and wave erosion at bay; and in addition to this protective function, this rich ecosystem functions as a breeding ground for fish and marine invertebrates, providing the necessary shelter for their eggs and larvae. It is also a significant economic resource for island dwellers, offering food, medicinal plants and wood. The economic value of a mangrove forest, including the income from fishing and tourism, and its protective function, is estimated at between $200,000 and $900,000 per square kilometre per year.

CRUISE SHIPS FITTED WITH SAILS USE LESS FUEL, GENERATE LESS GREENHOUSE EMISSIONS AND PROMOTE A MORE ECOLOGICAL FORM OF TOURISM.

In addition, as a veritable carbon storage system, the trees reduce CO_2 concentration in the atmosphere and so inhibit global warming. The services mangroves render to man and the environment are such that they have become a key factor in the quality of island life. Unfortunately the trees are often removed to make way for fish farms, or for charcoal production. However numerous replanting and protection programmes are now countering this trend.

As part of Samoa's Community Based Adaptation Small Grants Program, financed by the United Nations Programme for Development (UNPD) and the Samoan Ministry for the Environment, the women of the village of Vaiusu have launched their own mangrove replanting venture, summed up as follows by Ake Standley, president of the local Women's Committee: "We were given a choice of several projects and we opted for restoration of the mangrove swamps, which present all sorts of advantages for our village. The first aspect we looked into was the protection of coastal zones against wave and storm damage." More than 5,000 young mangroves have been planted, with a view to setting up a natural rampart between the village and the ocean.

The women of Vaiusu are also driven by the many economic benefits mangroves provide. They have realised that regeneration of the forest means improvements to their quality of life and their resources in all kinds of areas. "The mangrove forest," Ake Standley goes on, "is the place where little fish and crabs can grow to maturity because they're protected. Crabs are a favourite dish here, and when they're big enough we sell them and make some extra money. This is a real help for poor families. Another good point for us as mothers is that you can dye sarongs with the juice from the trees; we call them *ie tye dye*. We also use parts of the tree for medicinal purposes. And with the shells we gather in the forest, we make craft objects and necklaces to sell to tourists. When the wood is dry it burns very well and so we collect it to make fires or to sell. That's another part of making a living. And it really helps people who don't have a lot of money."

The members of the Women's Committee would like to enlarge the scope of their activities and are hoping for funding to expand ecotourism in the forest. Ake Standley bubbles with enthusiasm: "We're really keen on the idea. We could organize canoe trips, for example. And these are just some of the reasons why we put the replanting and preservation plan into action. We're very grateful to UNPD for the funding that helped us get the project under way.[39] We see this as a great long-term investment, as the mangrove provides all sorts of uses and advantages for our village, not to mention our country. We feel we've done something worthwhile that could serve as an example to the whole of Samoa."

FOLLOWING DOUBLE PAGE: MANGROVE ROOTS HOLD THE SEA-FLOOR TOGETHER
AND PROTECT TROPICAL COASTLINES. THESE INVALUABLE FORESTS ARE NOW BEING REGENERATED
BY NUMEROUS REPLANTING PROGRAMMES.

CARBON NEUTRALITY: ISLANDS SHOW THE WAY

TOURISM: CO_2 A GOGO

While tourism represents a vital market component for many islands, the problems it can pose are many: in terms not only of refuse, water consumption, pressure on the natural environment and impact on local cultures, but also increased greenhouse gas emissions. During the International Conference on Climate Change and Tourism in Davos, Switzerland, in 2007,[40] the participating states recognised that tourism is at once partly responsible for the climate crisis and extremely sensitive to its consequences. Once again, islands are the first to be affected: if coral reefs bleach and die, if beaches disappear, if the shortage of water becomes inconvenient and violent storms more frequent, visitors go looking for somewhere more restful. It is currently estimated that tourism accounts for around 5% of the world's carbon emissions. Transport – especially by plane – represents 75% of the total, but accommodation is also a significant energy consumer and thus a major contributor (20% of emissions) to the mounting greenhouse effect. The report of another conference in 2009[41] predicts that if there are no changes in tourism practices the emissions the industry is responsible for will increase by 135% by 2035. At the close of the conference, then, there seemed an urgent need for policies encouraging sustainable tourism, which incorporates climatic, environmental, social and economic concerns.

For this to happen the tourism sector must gradually reduce its greenhouse gas emissions from transport and accommodation, as well as improving its overall energy performance and providing technical and financial aid to help small island developing states adapt to climate change. At Davos countries like Sri Lanka stressed their desire to serve as examples in terms of carbon neutrality: preservation of their forests and other vegetation, which trap carbon, would mean they could compensate for their emissions. If they are to keep their tourist industries healthy, host countries must above all introduce innovative environmental management policies: protection of woodland and marine environments as carbon "wells", increased use of renewable energy, consumption of local produce in hotels and restaurants (to reduce transport-related emissions), recycling, energy-saving, etc. Some countries have introduced tourist taxes as a way of financing their anti-warming measures, and a host of other initiatives are also possible for reducing the impact of tourism: optimal passenger numbers in planes, for example, together with an emphasis on the most direct routes. Ships, buses and other less polluting modes of transport could also be used on a larger scale, and a number of cruise companies have already undertaken to reduce their greenhouse gas emissions by turning to more ecological methods of propulsion. To take one example, in 2000 fifteen members of the Florida-Caribbean Cruise Association, operating in the Caribbean, signed an agreement regarding the designing of more energy-efficient, less polluting ships.[42] Another initiative, the Caribbean Carbon Neutral Tourism Program, has been set up to enable funding of a number of projects, some focusing on renewable energy and energy efficiency in hotels, others on production of informative documentary films, and others still on promotion of ecotourism. Today the market, influenced by rising customer demand for preservation of the environment, is opening up to a responsible tourism, which could contribute to improved local living conditions and the fight against poverty.

ACTION AT ALL LEVELS

Ways of adapting to and mitigating climate change already exist, but the problem of funding remains. To take one example, the cost of protecting the coast of Jamaica in the event of a one-metre rise in sea level has been estimated at 462 million dollars per year, or 19% of the country's gross domestic product.[43] As was pointed out by Dessima Williams, until 2011 president of the Alliance of Small Island States (AOSIS), "We lack the money needed to tackle problems we did not cause and to which we have devoted our best efforts during twenty years of resistance and frustration. While our fate depends on the way we protect and conserve our oceans and our coastline, we are hampered by rising sea levels and a dearth of resources." Nonetheless, drawing on their own resources as well as international aid and regional partnerships, many projects have been set in motion at levels ranging from the local micro-initiative to the national and international. And given that there is no shortage of ideas, the years to come should see more and more innovative plans for adapting to climate change – even if it still remains to find the necessary funding. In France, for example, a competition has been launched by the Jacques Rougerie Foundation[44] and Nausicaá, the National Marine Centre, to reward designers of architectural solutions to the rising sea level problem. This is an opportunity for architects, designers, engineers and urbanists to focus on major contemporary issues in a context of increased environmental, industrial and technological responsibility. In the island context the number of anti-carbon emission initiatives is impressive. The green economy, recycling, and education and awareness programmes are taking shape everywhere, often thanks to pooling of skills and financial resources. The action being taken in the energy field is emblematic of islands' ecological commitment; this is one of the keys to their future, energy being much more expensive on islands than on the continents: in some island countries electricity is 500 times more expensive than in the United States! Moreover this dependency also has a social cost. In a context of climate crisis, islands have decided to make a real change by adopting energy policies that are responsible, ecological and job-generating. AOSIS members have just embarked on a twenty-year programme titled SIDS DOCK[45] aimed at a brand new energy policy for the Alliance of Small Island Developing States. The aim is creation of a collective mechanism to help member states transform their energy sectors; this would also act as a catalyst for sustainable economic development and generate additional income for climate change adaptation. These island countries hope that the plan will be conducive to mixed-economy partnerships and technology transfers. The stated goals are ambitious: compared to 2005, by 2033 50% of electricity should be coming from renewable sources, oil consumption should be cut by 20 to 30%, and energy efficiency should increase by 25%. By 2010 eleven countries had already signed a memorandum of understanding: the Bahamas, Belize, Cap Verde, Dominican Republic, Jamaica, Mauritius, the Palao Islands, St Lucia, Seychelles, the Solomon Islands and Grenada. Other nations – Barbados, Samoa, St Vincent and the Grenadines – have indicated their intention of joining them. SIDS DOCK's partners are the World Bank and the United Nations Programme for Development (UNPD). The action to be taken will involve grassroots experiments reproducible on a large scale. And so island states are now committed to providing an example in terms of the fight against global warming –while urging the big, most polluting countries to follow them.

SCHOOLS AGAINST GLOBAL WARMING IN SEYCHELLES

Brenda Andimignon is in charge of educational programmes at the Seychelles Ministry of the Environment. "The environmental priority here is climate change," she says. "Last year a spell of drought meant a water shortage, so we set up a climate change awareness programme explaining what we as individuals could do to adapt and not make things worse. We showed people model houses that demonstrate how you can live sustainably, save energy and consume without over-importing. We work with schools and the public."

A number of partners have committed to this agenda: the Education Department and NGOs like Sustainability for Seychelles, which runs awareness workshops for schools, and the Seychelles Wildlife Club – over 400 members, a branch in every school – which organises numerous projects and tackles a specific theme each year.

Adapting to the effects of global warming, which is already making itself felt in the archipelago, is a priority and schools are already hard at work: to cite one example, a pilot project for rainwater harvesting was carried out at the instigation of Jeannette Larue, environmental action coordinator for the Ministry of Education and the Ministry of the Environment.

"A secondary school set up a rainwater tank as part of a science project," Brenda Andimignon explains. "This got a lot of people interested and Jeannette Larue managed to get funding for material so that other schools could join in. Teachers and parents installed the tanks and the harvesting equipment, and now students use the water for watering the garden, washing the dishes – and drinking. A real success. The ten schools involved have seen their water bill drop considerably; one of them calculated an annual saving of $250, which is really something. And last year, a school in the south where the water is often cut off during the dry season had no problems. So the project has been really beneficial for schools."

Speaking and Acting Together

Small, but united by a sense of community, island states are striving to make themselves heard internationally. Together they represent a real political force and can defend their shared interests by pooling their skills and financial resources. One aim is to put pressure on the big continental countries to observe reasonable, responsible climate goals. Island states are calling on the world for solidarity and cooperation, but not as if they are welfare recipients. Their message is clear: all countries are concerned: humanity has a common destiny.

COMMON INTERESTS, SHARED REPRESENTATION

FROM RIO TO MAURITIUS: SEMINAL PROGRAMMES

At the first Earth Summit in Rio de Janeiro in 1992, islands were acknowledged by the international community as "a special case in environment and development terms". In the opinion of the representatives of all the world's nations, then, islands had "specific needs" – a status that was confirmed in more detail two years later at the Global Conference on the Sustainable Development of Small Island Developing States in Bridgetown, Barbados. That conference laid down a plan of action for making islands less vulnerable, fighting poverty and laying the groundwork for sustainable economic development. The priorities decided on included water management and preservation of natural resources – soil, forests, all-round biodiversity – together with health and education.

Eleven years later, in 2005, an international meeting in Mauritius brought the island states together again to evaluate the Barbados plan and make the necessary arrangements. Adopted unanimously, the Mauritius Strategy for the further implementation of the Programme of Action for the Sustainable Development of Small Island Developing States (SIDS) detailed nineteen action areas including refuse management, science, transport and communications, tourism, and trade. However, since the Barbados agreement, new and crucial issues have emerged. In the years before the Mauritius meeting a series of hurricanes had devastated the Caribbean and global warming-related phenomena such as enormous tides had become more and more frequent. Thus the main issue for the developing island

FOLLOWING DOUBLE PAGE: ISLANDS IN THE "CORAL TRIANGLE" BETWEEN INDONESIA, MALAYSIA AND THE PHILIPPINES ARE HOME TO THE WORLD'S GREATEST DIVERSITY OF MARINE SPECIES. WHILE REPRESENTING ONLY 1% OF THE EARTH'S SURFACE, THE AREA CONTAINS A THIRD OF ALL CORAL REEFS.

states was coping with climate change, followed by prevention of natural and environmental disasters. During the meeting Unesco director general Koichiro Matsuura reminded those present of islands' strong points: "There is also a need to stress the very special positive characteristics and strengths of small island nations and communities: their extraordinary capacity for adaptation and innovation; their proven determination and capability to overcome many adversities; their role as one of the world's front-line zones for addressing the challenges of sustainable development and sustainable living; and the recognized importance of maintaining solidarity among themselves while treasuring their diversity."[46] The emphasis was on cooperation between states, exchanges of experience and mobilisation of scientific institutions, political leaders and, more generally, skills and resources in island states and the world at large. Training and education were seen as crucial to meeting the objectives set by the Mauritius Strategy, together with communications as a means of involving all concerned – beginning with the citizens.

OPENED IN 2009, SEYCHELLES UNIVERSITY TRAINS STUDENTS IN THEIR HOMELAND, SPECIALISING IN THE FIELDS OF EDUCATION, MANAGEMENT, ICT AND ENVIRONMENTAL SCIENCE.

A CALL TO THE INTERNATIONAL COMMUNITY

To get their message across, small island states must speak in unison. Although they make up only some 5% of the world's population, they represent a real political force, as each has a voice at the United Nations, where the rule is "One country, one vote". In 1990 they formed a coalition to make their priorities known to the international community: the Alliance of Small Island States (AOSIS) comprises 43 countries from around the world, or 22% of the total UN membership of 192 nations. The aim of the alliance is to identify shared issues and the development programmes best suited to its members; it now obtains a better hearing internationally in respect of sustainable development, cooperation and solidarity, which means it can influence international negotiations and, hopefully, come up with better solutions to today's environmental, social and economic challenges.

AOSIS president until the end of 2011, Dessima Williams has been an indefatigable fighter for the interests of these small nations in the international context. In her speech at the opening of the *Histoires d'îles* ("Island Stories") exhibition at the Nausicaá marine centre in France in April 2011, she stressed the need for island unity in the face of enormous challenges: "They say that now we're equal to the big names in international forums, because we're united and we speak with a single voice." In her opinion, Ms Williams went on, 70% of the measures advocated by the Mauritius Strategy had been successfully carried out by AOSIS countries, and at the major international conferences and UN meetings they had made their aims clear on matters including food security, the fight against poverty, access to drinking water, health, climate, development and ocean management. However, she said, this was not enough: islands needed international solidarity and technical and financial aid. As she reminded her listeners, "The historic Earth Summit in Brazil in 1992, referred to in one report as the 'Generosity Summit', published Agenda 21. At the time the total annual cost of implementing Agenda 21 activities for sustainable development of small island countries was estimated at $130 million, including about $50 million from the international community on grant or concessional terms.[47] This estimate relates to the period 1993–2000 and the promised funding is still far from complete."

This, then, is the paradox: islands cannot isolate themselves from the rest of the world. They suffer the consequences of the development choices made by the big continental countries: not only greenhouse gas emissions, but also marine pollution, invasive species, loss of biodiversity, overexploitation of the sea's resources – and very often high prices for the basic necessities of life. The lives of island communities are also shaped by social and cultural change linked to the spread of the consumer society, globalisation and the tourism explosion; and this applies even to the remotest of them, in the furthest reaches of the ocean. Continents and islands share a single world in which everything is connected to everything else.

"WE ARE NOT ISOLATED" – AN APPEAL FROM ROLPH PAYET, MINISTER OF ENVIRONMENT, SEYCHELLES

Former president of the University of Seychelles and founder of the Sea Level Rise Foundation, before being named Minister of Environment in 2012, Rolph Payet comments, "When I was a child the sun rose and set on Seychelles and we had everything we needed. We used to think that our isolation meant we were immune to the world's problems and our Paradise would last forever. And now, for the last twenty years, we've been involved in global problems. We've witnessed the bleaching of coral, pollution of our waters by DDT that no one uses here, overfishing and pirate attacks along our coast. The Seychellois have realised that they're not isolated, and not protected from the impact of globalisation. My message to everybody is that there's no escaping from climate change: there's nowhere in the world where you can get away from it. On our islands we're like sentries, already feeling the effects. People on the continents and in the cities feel comfortable and protected, but they're going to feel the effects too, and believe me, it hurts. Because we all live together I'm asking the people of the world to activate programmes for energy saving, reduced fuel consumption, less refuse, and mitigation of pollution. Future generations have their eyes on us, and as consumers and decision makers we must take decisions that are in their interest. We want the children in our schools to grow up in a healthy, beautiful setting, in the kind of paradise Seychelles used to be."

CLIMATE NEGOTIATIONS: A UNITED FRONT

The big question now facing island micro-nations is climate change. And what is involved here for the Alliance of Small Island Developing States is nothing less than survival: "Despite their differences," insisted Dessima Williams at Nausicaá, "our 43 member states have one thing in common: we are highly vulnerable to economic shocks coming from outside and to climate change, and at the same time we are the least well equipped to deal with them. This is because of our small size, our open, dependent economies and our fragile infrastructures. Given the lack of really ambitious global policies and solidarity, most islands have no future to look forward to: many of them will not survive, or if they do, at the very least it will be at the cost of their territorial cohesion. Some of them have no more than 10,000 inhabitants, but they remain dynamic sovereign states, rooted in the specificity of their culture and identity."[48]

For some years now negotiations between countries on reductions in greenhouse gas emissions – attempts at agreement in the context of the United Nations Framework

Convention on Climate Change – have been extremely complicated. Each country defends its own interests, its own vision of the future and its own environmental concerns: from one summit to the next it is only with the greatest difficulty that a consensus is reached which, ultimately, seems to leave no one really satisfied. As a means of putting pressure on the international community, island states are joining forces to express their demands. Drawing on recent scientific reports, AOSIS has defined the maximum tolerance threshold for islands in terms of climate, and in 2009 it published its *Declaration on Climate Change*.[49] This text calls for limitation of global warming to 1.5°C above preindustrial levels, which means long-term stabilization of atmospheric greenhouse gas concentrations at well below 350 parts per million (ppm), being the pre-1990 figure. In February 2012 levels had already reached 393 ppm. AOSIS has also called for reduction of emissions starting in 2015. These demands are all the more restrictive in that the ceilings set by most industrialised countries allow for a maximum increase of 2°C and a concentration of greenhouse gases of up to 450 ppm.

Is anyone going to listen? The 2009 United Nations Climate Change Conference in Copenhagen, followed by those in Cancún (2010) and Durban (2011) failed to produce the restrictions AOSIS was hoping for, but a global greenhouse gas emissions pact is set for signing in 2015. It has also been decided to establish – in 2020 – an annual "green climate fund" of 100 billion dollars, to be financed by the developed countries as a means of helping developing nations to mitigate climate change and its consequences. The world's biggest economies are now having to face their responsibilities: long the main producers of greenhouse gases, the United States and Europe have now been equalled and even outstripped by emergent countries like China, India and Brazil. But must the growth of these economic giants be allowed to continue at the expense of micro-nations and the world's poorest countries, whose contribution to the present climate crisis is virtually nil? For AOSIS the issue is one of ethics and justice, and the message the alliance is now trying to get across is, "Island states are threatened by climate change for which, to a very large extent, they bear no responsibility. They are striving to adapt, but isolated action on their part is not enough. We need the entire world to adopt more ambitious climate and development policies, together with a new form of solidarity." (Declaration made by Dessima Williams, Nausicaà, France, 2011.)

ECOTOURISM STRESSES PRESERVATION OF THE ENVIRONMENT AND PROVIDES JOBS FOR LOCAL PEOPLE.
FARMLAND IN MALTA (TOP LEFT).
TRADITIONAL SALT PRODUCTION IN MALTA (BOTTOM LEFT).
DOLPHIN-WATCHING IN POLYNESIA (TOP RIGHT).
DIVING IN THE RED SEA: A MARINE MAMMAL, THE DUGONG (BOTTOM RIGHT)
IS NOW AN ENDANGERED SPECIES.

THE MOHÉLI MARINE PARK IN THE COMOROS: SEVERAL PROGRAMMES FOR MONITORING AND PRESERVING POPULATIONS OF DUGONG, TURTLES AND WHALES ARE CURRENTLY UNDER WAY.

ISLANDS AT THE CROSSROADS

NEW HORIZONS

For geographer and island expert Louis Brigand, islands have long been seen as exceptionally important by the governments of the world's most influential countries: "They have always had a strategic interest. They're outposts in times of war and so provide defence for the mainland. Down the centuries lots of them have been

armed or fortified. But if the enemy succeeds in capturing them, it has a perfect base for an attack. This is why the explorers first dropped anchor on the coastal islands of America and Asia, taking them over one by one before setting out to conquer the continent. They also work as relay stations, for telecommunications, for example, and the Americans and the French have used them as strategic bases, which is still the case today. However, new geopolitical issues have loomed larger and larger for islands in recent years: their location along the cargo routes for merchandise, oil, cereals and minerals; plus their marine territories, rich in living resources, minerals and energy; and their role as staging posts for undersea communications cables. In

THE SEA CUCUMBER IS AN INVERTEBRATE LIVING ON THE REEF IN MADAGASCAR.
A VICTIM OF OVER-HARVESTING, IT IS NOW RAISED IN MARINE PARKS AS PART OF A PROGRAMME INVOLVING LOCAL AND BELGIAN INSTITUTIONS, A PRIVATE COMPANY AND AN NGO.

the deep waters surrounding certain islands – Seychelles, for instance – the search for undersea oil reserves is going full speed ahead. Economic growth in Asia is pushing up both demand and prices, and as detection and extraction technologies become increasingly sophisticated, the quest for hydrocarbons, metals and rare minerals is going further and further afield: requests for prospecting permits by companies in search of polymetallic nodules and precious minerals are increasing every year. At the same time marine biodiversity, which is still little understood – especially in its deep-water varieties – is also opening up vast new horizons for biotechnology

and medicine. In 2010 investigations by the French Research Institute for Exploration of the Sea (IFREMER) in the exclusive economic zone of Wallis and Futuna, included prospecting for mineral resources and an inventory of the biodiversity in the hydrothermal sites[50] near the undersea volcano Kulolasi. This initiative was a joint venture involving public sector bodies – the Ministry of Sustainable Development, the French Agency for Marine Protected Areas, the Bureau of Geological and Mining Research (BRGM) – and a number of private companies.

The potential wealth of the sea depths is going to become a major global issue and could represent a new source of revenue and employment for island communities.

REPRODUCTION OF SEA CUCUMBERS IS DONE IN HATCHERIES, AN ADVANCED TECHNOLOGY DEVELOPED IN MADAGASCAR.

At the same time the ecological dangers are very real: pollution or degradation of the ocean floor would affect islanders' food sources and the local fishing and tourist industries, with extremely serious consequences. Good conduct codes are necessary for prospection and exploitation, but will they suffice on their own? Moreover, as islands lack the financial wherewithal to make the most of these assets, they will have no choice but to work in partnership with foreign powers and multinationals.

Harnessing of renewable energy is also opening up new technological and economic prospects, while fitting with sustainable development criteria and favouring autonomy for the islands in question. This is going hand in hand with forms of tourism that guarantee the long-term preservation of ecosystems and offer recompense for the "services" provided by nature; this is now a sector that can help fund sustainable management programmes for natural settings and resources. Recourse to land biodiversity as a "genetic bank" in the biological and medical spheres – natural drugs, essential oils and substances for use in pharmacology and the food and cosmetics industries – also hold out promise of new resources and economic activities, providing measures are taken to ensure that local people get their part of the profits.

Every day now island communities are demonstrating the potential of innovative development ventures. "To talk

APPROPRIATE EDUCATION AND TRAINING ARE VITAL TO IMPROVING ENVIRONMENTAL MANAGEMENT.
IN MADAGASCAR (TOP), HAITI (MIDDLE PHOTOS) AND THE MALDIVES (BOTTOM),
CHILDREN ARE LEARNING ABOUT THE WORLD AROUND THEM AND ITS SUBTLE BALANCES.

about islands in a general way is a very complicated business," comments Louis Brigand. "For every example there's a counter-example. But maybe that's the big asset. I've noticed that islands have always managed to adapt to worldwide social change – and in fact they've always been ahead of the game. They function in cycles to some extent, and anticipate what's going to happen on the continent. This points up their interest as laboratories."

COOPERATION AS A LAUNCH PAD FOR DEVELOPMENT

Generally speaking progress in small island states makes itself felt in social terms. In most of these countries access to drinking water is improving, infant mortality is falling and malnutrition is declining,[51] but poverty, unemployment, lack of education and environmental degradation remain major areas of concern. Improving quality of life requires commitment not only from all levels of society – politicians, economic actors, public figures, educators, scientists and ordinary citizens – but also from a world that recognises the right to greater solidarity and equity. In 2000 the Earth Charter discussed at the Rio Summit in 1992, was finally approved by Unesco as a declaration of fundamental principles for a just, sustainable and peaceful world society: "We stand at a critical moment in Earth's history, a time when humanity must choose its future. As the world becomes increasingly interdependent and fragile, the future at once holds great peril and great promise. To move forward we must recognize that in the midst of a magnificent diversity of cultures and life forms we are one human family [...] with a common destiny." The difficulties facing island countries, like those affecting developing countries as a whole, share their causes with trends to be found in the rest of the world. The resultant effects – poverty, degradation of the environment, emigration – in turn have repercussions on the planet as a whole and the entire world community. Everything is interconnected... As a way of dealing with the scientific, technological, economic and social challenges of the new millennium, island states have settled on a major two-part priority: use of their human resources and development of local skills. This is a matter, then, not only of training the men and women who will oversee development policy and its implementation, but also of working for autonomy and responsibility in all spheres and at all levels. Indispensable to this approach are dialogue, public/private partnerships, international cooperation and technology transfers. This is an approach that is valid anywhere, in any context. In Madagascar, for example, a collaborative venture involving the Madagascar Institute for Fishing and Marine Science (IHSM), two Belgian universities (the Free University of Brussels and the University of Mons-Hainaut), the private local company Holothurie SA and the French NGO Transmad' Développement, has led to the patenting of a

FOLLOWING DOUBLE PAGE: VALETTA, IN MALTA, IS ONE OF THE HANDSOMEST NATURAL PORTS IN EUROPE, AND TESTIMONY TO THE HISTORY OF THE MEDITERRANEAN. THE CITY TOOK SHAPE WHEN THE KNIGHTS OF MALTA MOVED THERE IN 1530.

reproduction method for sea cucumbers. Genetically related to the starfish and the sea urchin, these creatures live in the shallow waters of the island's coral reef, where they make a vital contribution to the ecological health of their surroundings by consuming the organic particles contained in the sand of the sea floor. Certain varieties of sea cucumber are capable of "cleaning" hundreds of metric tons of sand annually, but they are considered a delicacy in Asia and are bought from local fishermen by exporters for resale at outrageous prices. Overfishing had led to a marked decline in the sea cucumber population, the upshot being deterioration of the reef and the departure of many fish. However, the innovative technique developed by local and Belgian researchers has led to an increase in egg fertilisation and year-round larvae production. The eggs are taken to a hatchery, and the resultant larvae to a fish farm where they are raised in tanks. Once they have reached a length of around 8 centimetres, they are passed on to local fishermen, who let them grow to a minimum of 20 centimetres in pens in the sea, then sell them. This means the fishermen have a source of income without having to strip the reef of its wild sea cucumbers, whose renewed populations are restoring the vitality of the ecosystem. This exemplary initiative means success for a local business, income for the fishermen, preservation of an important feature of the environment – and maybe inspiration for other projects elsewhere.

MAKING THE MOST OF SCIENCE

In the scientific field, knowledge sharing and research dissemination are an important part of making realistic choices for the future. Creation of international bodies like the Intergovernmental Panel on Climate Change (IPCC) in 1998 and the Intergovernmental Science Policy Platform on Biodiversity and Ecosystem Services (IPBES) in 2010 give everyone access to information and predictions regarding changes to the global environment. The Intergovernmental Oceanographic Commission (IOC-Unesco) sets up international programmes for the dissemination of scientific information (see box, page 225), while international partnerships between government research bodies have also given rise to shared programmes in many island-related scientific fields. Finding funding for research and development ventures concerning energy, biodiversity, health, information technology, water management and a host of other subjects is fundamental for island states which depend on cooperation with big countries to compensate for their lack of technical and human resources.

INTERNATIONAL COOPERATION AND THE STUDY OF OUR OCEANS

As Doctor Wendy Watson-Wright, assistant director-general of Unesco and executive secretary of the Intergovernmental Oceanographic Commission (IOC-Unesco), sees it, "We have to accept the fact that there are not several oceans, but just a single one, since they all intercommunicate. What affects one marine region also affects all the others. Fish migrate from one sea to another and currents transport larvae, nutrition, warmth and pollution. There are no political or geographic borders here. The ocean is a key component of the climate system, controlling its changes and variability via exchange with the atmosphere. It also absorbs carbon dioxide resulting from human activities and, as a result, becomes more acidic, and this can affect the marine ecosystems we depend on. People have their own impacts on the ocean: pollution, nutrition input, fishing, use of resources, etc. The ocean belongs to all of us and suffers the consequences of our actions." Whence the importance of an international alliance for scientific research into the ocean; but this global cooperation means accepting that not all nations can make the same technical and financial contributions, nor provide the same skills: "Many nations have the means to undertake ocean observation and research, so cooperation and coordination allow each country, however modest its contribution, to benefit from the work of all. Governments, though, are only interested in what happens within their jurisdiction. This is why international cooperation and coordination are absolutely essential to a global view of things: without this interaction problems cannot be solved. Climatic and oceanographic data must be shared, since purely national information cannot provide a global perspective."

The IOC-Unesco is devoted to the oceanographic sciences: study of the effects of climate change on oceans, marine ecosystems and the ecological services they render, as well as direct impacts on human populations. Its observations enable a better understanding of the "ocean system" in all its complexity. This means, too, that political decision-makers have access to optimal data and predictive information. In a context of climate change these projections provide invaluable information for different sectors and communities and are essential to sound decision-making and the implementation of policies of adaptation and mitigation: "I am proud of IOC-Unesco's decisive role in instigating the first global-scale programme of research into environmental change: the World Climate Research Programme (WCRP), now considered exemplary. As regards to adaptation and mitigation, IOC-Unesco is intensifying its efforts within WCRP and moving from a global to a regional scale: this is a way of honing impact studies of climate models. This is particularly important for

FOLLOWING DOUBLE PAGE: BRINGING HOME THE CATCH ON THE ISLAND OF KULHUDHUFFUSHI IN THE MALDIVES.

developing countries, where these studies help national bodies working in the fields of oceanography, safety, climate change, ecosystems, tourism, etc. I would like to emphasise that for the programmes developed by IOC-Unesco to be successful, commitment by member countries is vital. They have to have a sense of belonging to the Commission. Our programmes are enhanced, too, by the active participation of our partner bodies in the scientific and awareness fields. And needless to say, it's very important to be able to count on stable, regular funding."

FROM ISLAND TO ISLAND: POOLING KNOWLEDGE AND SKILLS

As Grenada's prime minister Thomas Tillman put it in New York in 2009, "The unique characteristics and vulnerability of small island states are an encouragement to exchanges of experience: of lessons learned, sound initiatives and indigenous skills adapted to island ways of life." So while island states count on collaboration and technology transfers with the world's great powers, they are also looking to networking between islands: communication of observations and data, exchanges of good ideas, sharing experiments that work, passing on information. Inter-island networking, which enables pooling of grey matter, technical resources and funding, has developed considerably and in a number of different forms. The Internet has made possible networks like SIDSnet,[52] the Small Islands Developing States Network, which publishes information on, among other things, international summits, declarations relating to island states, the latest reports and scientific studies, and programmes in progress. Above all this is an effective tool for promoting contacts and partnerships and presenting successful experiments communities would like to share. To facilitate exchange and cooperation, Unesco has also created the Intersectoral Platform for Small Island Developing States as a means of inventorying and expanding projects (see interview on the facing page).

«

Encouraging dialogue: expanding and coordinating island action.

Interview with Hans Thulstrup, Unesco

HANS THULSTRUP, A PROGRAMME SPECIALIST AT UNESCO, TALKS ABOUT THE INTERSECTORAL PLATFORM FOR SMALL ISLAND DEVELOPING STATES, SET UP TO COORDINATE UNESCO'S ROLE IN IMPLEMENTATION OF THE MAURITIUS STRATEGY.[53]

What are the platform's main objectives?

By putting the emphasis on interregional relations and cooperation, the platform enables an integrated, interdisciplinary approach. Drawing on the whole gamut of Unesco exercise, it aims at meeting island societies' expectations in terms of inventiveness and determination. It coordinates and promotes Unesco activities for its 44 member states and their associates. And to make sure the programmes and activities are meeting real needs, Unesco regularly exchanges information with the island states' Committee of Representatives.

What are the main challenges facing small island developing states. And how can international cooperation contribute to meeting them?

Today's challenges are unprecedented. In an increasingly globalised and interconnected world, and one subject to climatic and financial crises, small islands are particularly in danger because of ever more violent and unpredictable weather, their low altitude, their geographic isolation and the vulnerability of their economies.

What fields does the platform mainly take action in?

Climate change is a priority issue and one of the greatest challenges facing islands: it affects ways of life, resources, cultures and societies, and is a threat to the very existence of low-altitude countries. Unesco is backing joint action in terms of climate change research and education, one example being the Sandwatch programme, which has students and teachers from 25 island nations monitoring and analysing their coastal environments.

Unesco has created the Climate Frontlines website to facilitate sharing of observations, experiences and innovation between islands, indigenous peoples and other vulnerable communities affected by climate change.

That way their voices and concerns will be heard in international debate on the subject. The platform also stresses cultural and natural heritages, skill enhancement, and sustainable management of water and sea and land resources, as well as focusing on prevention and management of natural and environmental disasters.

How is the international community concerned by the issues facing small island states? And how can it contribute to dealing with them?

Every country has something to learn from what is happening on small islands. Understanding the way environmental changes affect them gives a better idea of the phenomenon on a larger scale. In the same way islands' ventures in adaptation and mitigation provide vital lessons that need to be communicated to the rest of the world. This means, too, that small islands – with the support of the international community – are making a major contribution to sustainable development and by extension to the future of all of us.

COMMON INTERESTS AT REGIONAL LEVEL

Other initiatives are based on a regional or thematic approach to island development issues. The Global Island Partnership (GLISPA), for example, concentrates on preservation and sustainable utilisation of biodiversity, and is taking part in implementation of the work programme for the islands prepared by the Convention on Biological Diversity (CBD): it helps with setting up partnerships and obtaining funding for grassroots action. Having no actual structure or team – just an official coordinator – GLISPA functions as an informal network, providing advice and backing for biodiversity activities and initiatives that emphasise sustainable use of biological resources and reduction of damage to natural settings. It notably supports extension of protected area networks and the fight against invasive species (see page 88).

With regard to the regional approach, several bodies involved in island development programmes have been set up in the Caribbean, the Pacific, and the Indian Ocean. The Secretariat of the Pacific Community (SPC) provides technical, scientific and strategic aid for islands in Oceania through assistance, information and research units. Its aim is sustainable development in the economic, environmental, human and social sectors and it is involved in a host of projects in fields including energy, transport, fishing, forest management, agriculture, public health, climate change adaptation, information technology, and help with strategy and planning. The Indian Ocean Commission is another regional body embracing the Comoros, Madagascar, La Réunion, Seychelles and Mauritius. It defends its members' interests at the political, economic and trade levels, and promotes human development and sustainable environmental management. Working on a cooperative basis, it seeks solutions to exposure to natural disasters, isolation, restricted markets and environmental vulnerability, while also taking action in sectors as varied as legal assistance and the setting up of agreements regarding safety, networking of intervention in the event of natural disasters, community management of fishing (surveillance, monitoring of tuna populations), IT backup, cultural cooperation and support for farmers adapting to climate change.

TRAINING AND EDUCATION: INVESTING IN THE FUTURE

SCHOOLS AND UNIVERSITIES: LAYING THE GROUNDWORK

Building universities specialising in every major field, plus paying for teaching personnel, laboratories and educational, scientific and computer equipment is beyond the reach of the smallest states. With a view to increasing local skills, some island states have pooled their resources. Financed by Spain, the University Consortium of Small Island States (UCSIS) comprises the Universities of the South Pacific, the Western Antilles, the American Virgin Islands, Mauritius and Malta. Two others – the universities of Las Palmas and Seychelles – may join in the future. A Master's degree in sustainable development for island states is currently in preparation and the courses will go out on the Internet, making them accessible to students at all the member universities. This study programme is being put together by inventorying the courses and technical resources of each participating institution.

But public awareness begins at primary school. And once again islands have demonstrated their creativity: how many big countries can boast of having integrated environmental education into all school subjects at both primary and secondary level. In Seychelles trainee teachers take a mandatory module in ecological awareness, which they then have to integrate into their teaching. A mathematics teacher, for example, will have her pupils draw up statistical charts based on the study of bird populations; a language teacher will choose a text on nature preservation; and the biology class will involve creating a garden and learning to identify endangered and protected species. Thus the environment slots naturally into the curriculum.

In island countries without this system, sustainable development awareness for students is often the concern of local or international bodies, with initiatives making their appearance everywhere: knowing your natural setting and its fauna and flora; ecology for all; responsible environmental conduct; discovery trails; diving and other activities. In French Polynesia Cécile Gaspar, co-founder of the World Ocean Network, chairs the Te Mana o Te Moana association, which introduces children to the natural wonders of the Pacific isles. With backing from private sector partners she organises educational activities involving turtles, dolphins and coral reefs. Teaching kits mean these programmes go out to as many schools as possible. In Samoa the American body Ocean Futures Society distributes a "sustainable reef" teaching kit comprising a comic book, a film, game ideas and other material for teachers and pupils in Samoan and English.

At regional level the Indian Ocean Commission's "Arpeggio" project distributes teaching kits and manuals. Combining these ventures internationally and letting everyone benefit from everyone else's experience is proving an effective method of increasing their impact. The Unesco-backed Sandwatch programme started with the idea of providing schools, community associations and local institutions with tools for evaluating climate change impact on coastlines and taking the necessary counter-measures. Launched in the Caribbean in 2001, it now extends to the Pacific and Indian Ocean communities. A feature of the project is a manual for monitoring beaches – erosion, water quality, garbage, fauna and flora – which has also gone out to local workers in the field. The Sandwatch website[54] lets internauts compare experiments even when these have been carried out on islands very far apart.

AZEEZ ABDUL HAKEEM, HEAD OF THE MARINE LAB ON THE ISLAND OF VABBINFARU IN THE MALDIVES, HAS CREATED A NATURE PARK WHERE SHARKS ARE CAPTURED, MARKED AND RELEASED WITH A VIEW TO MONITORING THEIR POPULATIONS AND THEIR BEHAVIOUR.

GRASSROOTS EDUCATION

Very much aware that their countries' futures hinge on conservation of their environment and technological, social and human development, island state governments are encouraging sustainable development education and awareness at all levels of society. Most closely concerned are those who earn their living directly from the environment – farmers, forestry workers, fishermen and people from the tourism, town planning, energy and territorial development sectors – and their participation is vital in terms of meeting stated sustainability objectives. Nature preservation campaigns, for example, cannot be carried through without the support of the communities who know the setting intimately and gain their livelihood from it. And so projects of this kind are striving more and more for direct involvement, as in the creation of Marine Protected Areas (see page 147).
In this context communication is a vital tool for optimal dissemination of information and an understanding of what is at stake in sound resource management. In Indonesia a large-scale government campaign has been organised to ensure the management and preservation of the Raja Ampat Islands and the world's largest sample of marine biodiversity. Situated in the "coral triangle" between the Solomon Islands, Indonesia and the Philippines, this natural wonderland is home to more

MOORÉA IN FRENCH POLYNESIA: CÉCILE GASPAR, VETERINARIAN AND DIRECTOR OF THE TE MANA O TE MOANA COMMUNITY ASSOCIATION, RELEASES A GREEN SEA TURTLE AFTER TREATMENT IN A SPECIAL CENTRE.

than 1,000 species of fish and 537 of coral. The preservation measures are financed by a tax levied on divers and tourists. Local fishermen contribute to management of the reef via the "Symbiosis" project's awareness programme, and films shot in Indonesian[55] with local actors are shown in villages and schools. In the Comoros the Swiss Cetacean Society (SCS) has adopted the same approach for a turtle protection programme in the Mohéli marine reserve: a film in the local language is shown in the villages to alert fishermen to the environmental consequences of poaching and the rules to be obeyed if turtle populations are to be reconstituted and are to return to lay their eggs on the beaches. Countless ventures like these are now under way on islands all over the world. Thanks to the work of associations and government and international bodies, there has been a rapid spread of sustainability awareness – learning, understanding, participating – in recent years. People are committing to a better future for all, impelled by an urge to improve their lives and to use progress and solidarity to avoid social regression in an irretrievably damaged environment.

INFORMATION AND EXPERIENCE SHARING IN THE MEDITERRANEAN

France's Coastal Protection Agency is a public body whose objective is to acquire and manage ecologically threatened sections of the nation's shoreline. It also coordinates the Small Mediterranean Islands initiative and is contributing to protection of these micro-spaces via concrete on-site measures and encouragement of knowledge and skills exchanges between experts and the various managers of the Mediterranean basin as a whole. As Fabrice Bernard, the Coastal Protection Agency's European and international delegate, explains, "One of the main aims is to develop local know-how. The agency has been around for more than thirty-five years now, and has real experience in integrated management of coastal zones. And islands are very good places to learn: all the main themes are there – preservation of biodiversity, impact of human activity, climate change, etc. – and the scale means you can take concrete action and evaluate its effects. We see international exchanges as a very important way of sharing what we learn, while at the same time improving our skills and training methods. This is why we set up the Pharos and Island Workshops programmes."

"Pharos" began with the realisation that although lots of information was available about Mediterranean islands, it was scattered and hard to access. Centralising it would mean that scientists, managers and people involved in island life could use it to start or improve their own projects. Pharos is a database offering accurate information about different islands – geographical details, environmental characteristics, legal status, regulations, living species, etc. – not only to specialists, but to the general public as well. It also provides an online library and information and awareness material in the form of booklets, exhibitions, logbooks, and so on.

The Islands Workshop programme also has to do with knowledge and experience sharing, with field missions being organised on subjects relating to island management: "Since 2005," says Fabrice Bernard, "these hands-on training projects have enabled comparisons between the experience and know-how of all sorts of specialists and in-the-field personnel from six other Mediterranean countries. In Tunisia and Algeria, for example, ecoguards and site supervisors have been trained to eradicate invasive species, monitor the flora and fauna, keep track of visitors and more generally learn the métier of coastline protection. These practical educational projects mean expertise can be handed on via concrete action such as bird counts, path creation, cartography, building restoration, refuse management and public awareness – all things you need to know about as a nature reserve manager and coastline guard." This kind of international cooperation for an entire sea needs to be expanded and could serve as an example to other parts of the world.

COORDINATED BY FRANCE'S COASTAL PROTECTION AGENCY, THE SMALL MEDITERRANEAN ISLANDS INITIATIVE ORGANISES GRASSROOTS ECOLOGICAL ACTIVITIES AND EXCHANGES OF KNOWLEDGE AND SKILLS.
THE SUGITON *CALANQUE*, NEAR MARSEILLE (TOP LEFT).
FORMER SALT MARSHES IN THE BRUSC LAGOON ON EMBIEZ ISLAND, OFF TOULON, FRANCE (TOP RIGHT).
SMALL-SCALE FISHING OFF EMBIEZ ISLAND, FRANCE (BOTTOM LEFT).
A DUSKY GROUPER FROM THE MEDITERRANEAN (BOTTOM RIGHT).

A SCHOOL OF ANTHIAS IN THE MEDITERRANEAN.

PAGE 238 TOP: FISHERMAN AND BOYS IN MADAGASCAR.
PAGE 238: BOTTOM: BOYS IN SEYCHELLES.
PAGE 239: GIRLS IN THE MALDIVES.

Towards a Blue Society

"What we do with respect to small islands has implications far beyond their troubled shores. By working with small islands on their problems, we can find solutions for ours. Brighter horizons for small islands can mean brighter horizons for the world in general."

(United Nations Secretary-General Kofi Annan,
addressing the Special Session of the United Nations General Assembly
on sustainable development for small islands,
27 September 1999.)

Islands of promise, outpost islands, lighthouse islands, in the immensity of our planet's oceans. Confronted with enormous continental landmasses and the great powers of this world, islands are often the poor relatives on the international scene: recipients of a sympathetic smile, triggers for a fleeting moment of pleasure or fantasy probably clicking in from childhood, as if we already know all there is to be known. Yet islands deserve more reflection about their future: places of transit and interchange, they are a melting pot where a new relationship between man and the ocean is taking shape. In the forefront when it comes to facing today's big global challenges, they represent the perfect terrain for sustainable development initiatives. At the dawn of a new millennium and in a context of worldwide economic and environmental crisis, humanity is being offered a great opportunity: the creation of a less predatory, more ethical, more responsible society. We have come to the realisation that we are living in a finite world, that our resources are limited and that our activities have a serious impact on the natural heritage we depend on. Island dwellers have known this for a long time; and together with them we can weigh up our needs for the future while respecting the natural balances essential to our survival.

In the final analysis, are we not all island dwellers? Is not the Earth an inhabited island lost in space? The ocean that covers almost three-quarters of our planet is home to millions of different species ranging from microorganisms to whales, and provides indispensable living and mineral resources. The ocean regulates our climate, plays its part in the water cycle, produces half the oxygen we breathe and recycles nutrients. Island dwellers, long accustomed to being surrounded by water, have integrated this vital link with the sea into their cultures and ways of life. For us, now, the ocean remains the ultimate space for exploration, with all its enormous scientific, technological, economic and environmental potential. It is by looking to the ocean that we will discover new resources, innovative solutions and life-enhancing experiences. A "Blue Society" could be born out of our collective endeavour: out of the belief that equity and sustainability can ensure a better future.

Notes

1- Statement at the fifth Global Oceans Conference in Paris in May 2010.
2- A teacher-researcher in geography at the University of Western Brittany (UBO), Louis Brigand works with a number of bodies – UNESCO, the Conservatoire du Littoral (Shoreline Conservation Agency) and the French Marine Protected Areas Agency – as well as networks dedicated to islands. Over the last thirty years he has written numerous articles and books on the subject.
3- Local and Indigenous Knowledge Systems.
4- Open to all United Nations member countries, the IPCC assesses the risks involved in human-induced climate change, its possible consequences and mitigation strategies.
5- *Enhancing the Climate Risk and Adaptation Fact Base for the Caribbean*, CCRIF, 2010.
6- *Haïti: résumé du PDNA du tremblement de terre. Evaluation sectorielle des dommages, des pertes et des besoins. La catastrophe et ses impacts*, report prepared by the Haitian government with the backing of the international community, 2010.
7- Coordinated internationally by World Ocean Network.
8- These include the Regional Cooperation Fund, the Nature et Découvertes Foundation, the Lemarchand Foundation, the Conservatoire Botanique des Antilles Françaises, Apigua, Mon École/Ma Baleine and the Whitley Fund for Nature.
9- Charles Darwin, *The Voyage of the Beagle* (New York: Dover, 2011), 398.
10- Ibid, 381.
11- Philibert Commerson, letter to Jérôme de Lalande, astronomer and member of France's Royal Academy of Science, 18 April 1771.
12- Holder of a PhD in geography and a university teacher, Christophe Lefebvre worked for France's Coastal Protection Agency before becoming a delegate to the European and International section of the Marine Protected Areas Agency. He is also president of the French Committee of the International Union for Conservation of Nature (IUCN) and IUCN adviser to World Ocean Network.
13- "Assises Méditerranéennes des Petites Iles", Six-Fours, France, 7–10 October 2009. See A. Zenetos and N. Streftaris, *Number of Aliens in European Seas*, 2008.
14- "Assises Méditerranéennes des Petites Iles", op. cit.
15- Jon Barnett and John Campbell, *Climate Change and Small Island States – Power, Knowledge and the South Pacific* (London: Routledge, 2010).
16- Known locally as the *bourgeois* or the *vivaneau*, the Emperor Red Snapper *(Lutjanus sebae)* is among the Seychelles' most appreciated table fish.
17- A cork-floated line fitted with hooks.
18- FAO National Fisheries Sector overview – Maldives, http://www.fao.org/fishery/countrysector/FI-CP_MV/en.
19- Ibid.
20- The United Nations Rio+20 Conference is the fifth Earth Summit. These summits are held every ten years, the most recent being those in Rio de Janeiro in 1992 (whence the term Rio+20) and the Sustainable Development Summit in Johannesburg in 2002.
21- The Global Forum on Oceans, Coasts and Islands was created during the Johannesburg Summit in 2002, as a means of stimulating government and civil society action. See http://www.globaloceans.org/
22- CRISP press release, Brasilia, 1st August 2010: "The Little Nation That Could and Did: Kiribati's Phoenix Islands Protected Area earns global spotlight as largest World Heritage site on Earth".
23- *Challenges and Emerging Issues in Agriculture, Forestry and Fisheries*, Paper prepared by FAO on the occasion of the Inter-Regional Conference of Small Island Developing States, Bahamas, 26–30 January 2004.
24- Brochure about PRERURE, Regional Energy Control programme.
25- ARER is a non-profit body founded in 2000 at the instigation of the Réunion Regional Council, the Council for Culture, Education and the Environment (CCEE), the Regional Economic, Social and Environmental Council (CESER), the Ademe energy agency and Electricité de France, via the Regional Energy Control Programme (PRME) and PRERURE.
26- Founded in 2005, the Alofa Tuvalu association has launched its "Small is Beautiful" campaign to increase awareness of the need to reduce greenhouse gas emissions and to work at finding local ways of adapting to the consequences of climate change. See its site: http://alofatuvalu.tv/
27- *UNEP and Small Island Developing States: 1994 to 2004 and Future Perspectives*. United Nations Environment Programme, Nairobi, 2004.
28- *UNWTO World Tourism Barometer*, vol. 8, no. 1, January 2010.
29- Virginie Duvat, "Mondialisation touristique et environnement dans les petites îles tropicales", *Les Cahiers d'outre-mer* [http://com.revues.org/], no. 236, October–December 2006.
30- Report of the United Nations Secretary General, *Protection of Coral Reefs for Sustainable Livelihoods and Development*, 12 August 2011
31- Reef Check is a non-profit international organisation devoted to coral reef preservation. Its headquarters are in California, but its volunteers are at work in 80 countries.
32- The Atmospheric Radiation Measurement (ARM) Climate Research Facility is responsible to the American Department of Energy. http://www.arm.gov/
33- Established in 1970, NOAA analyses, predicts and makes public changes in the marine and atmospheric environments. Its work puts particular emphasis on the prediction and study of storms, climate, fishing management and coastline preservation.
34- Founded in 2005, this French-Tuvaluan association organises local programmes for limiting greenhouse gas emissions. http://www.alofatuvalu.tv/
35- Tuvalu Overview has branches in Tuvalu and Tokyo. http://tuvalu-overview.tv
36- This project has been undertaken in conjunction with the Hidenori Watanabe Laboratory at Tokyo Metropolitan University.
37- The event was recorded by documentary film maker Briar March in *There Once Was an Island: Te Henua e Nnoho*, On The Level Productions, www.thereoncewasanisland.com.
38- "Unesco Declares Baa Atoll a Biosphere Reserve", in *Voices*, UNDP Maldives Newsletter, Issue #1, August 2011. http://www.undp.org.mv/v2/?lid=202.
39- *Tofiga O Pili Aau*, a film made by InsightShare with a group of a dozen Samoans, provides an interesting picture of initiatives involving vulnerable communities and their efforts at limiting the impact of climate change on their environment, way of life and infrastructures.
40- World Tourism Organisation, *From Davos to Bali: A Tourism Contribution to the Challenge of Climate Change*, 2007.
41- World Tourism Organisation, *From Davos to Copenhagen and Beyond: Advancing Tourism's Response to Climate Change*, Background Paper.
42- M. C. Simpson, S. Gössling, D. Scott, C. M. Hall and E. Gladin, *Climate Change Adaptation and Mitigation in the Tourism Sector: Frameworks, Tools and Practices*, United Nations Environment Programme, 2008.
43- *Climate Change, Small Island Developing States*, Climate Change Secretariat, United Nations Framework Convention on Climate Change (UNFCCC), Bonn, 2005.
44- Architect Jacques Rougerie set up the Centre for Marine and Space Architecture in 1974, before going on to found the Jacques Rougerie Architectes Associés agency.
45- SIDS DOCK has been jointly drawn up by the Caribbean Community Climate Change Centre (CCCCC) and the Secretariat of the Pacific Regional Environment Programme (SPREP).
46- Koïchiro Matsuura, director general of Unesco, at the plenary session of the international meeting in Mauritius, 13 January 2005.
47- Agenda 21, chapter 17.
48- Statement made by Dessima Williams, Grenada's ambassador to the United Nations and former president of the Alliance of Small Island States at the opening of the exhibition "Islands' Stories", on 15 April 2011 at Nausicaá, the Centre national de la Mer at Boulogne-sur-Mer.
49- Alliance of Small Island States (AOSIS), *Declaration on Climate Change*, 2009.
50- Areas where extremely hot, mineral-rich water gushes up from the sea bed.
51- United Nations, *Trends in Sustainable Development: Small Island Developing States*, New York, 2010.
52- http://www.sidsnet.org/
53- The Mauritius Strategy, of 2005, for further the implementation of the Barbados plan for Sustainable Development of SIDS.
54- http://www.sandwatch.ca
55- The films are the work of French filmmaker Sébastien Thiébot.

Selected Bibliography

BOOKS

AUTISSIER Isabelle and DAUDET Lionel, *Versant océan: l'île du bout du monde*, Grasset, Paris, 2008.

AUTISSIER Isabelle and ORSENNA Erik, *Salut au grand Sud*, Stock, Paris, 2006.

BALDACCHINO Godfrey (edited by), *A World of Islands*, Institute of Island Studies, University of Prince Edward Island, Canada, and Agenda Academic, Malta, 2007.

BARNETT Jon and CAMPBELL John, *Climate Change and Small Island States: Power, Knowledge and the South Pacific (Earthscan Climate)*, London, Routledge, 2010.

DARWIN Charles, *The Voyage of the Beagle*, New York, Dover, 1992 (1st published in 1839).

DEHOORNE Olivier and SAFFACHE Pascal (edited by), *Mondes insulaires tropicaux : géopolitique, économie et développement durable*, multiple authors. "Carrefours, les dossiers", Ellipses, Paris, 2008.

DUVAT Virginie and MAGNAN Alexandre, *Ces îles qui pourraient disparaître*, Le Pommier, Paris, 2012.

FOLLIET Luc, *Nauru, l'île dévastée: comment la civilisation capitaliste a détruit le pays le plus riche du monde*, La Découverte, Paris, 2009.

SCIENTIFIC PUBLICATIONS

AGENCE RÉGIONALE DE L'ÉNERGIE RÉUNION (ARER), *Bilan énergétique de l'île de la Réunion 10*, Observatoire énergie Réunion éditions, 2011.
BOUCHARD Christian, "Transition énergétique dans le contexte des petits Etats et territoires insulaires", département de géographie de l'Université laurentienne, *Actes de la 15e Journée Sciences et Savoirs*, Acfas, Sudbury (ON), 2009, pp. 197–211.

BOUCHON Claude and BOUCHON-NAVARO Yolande, *Invasion de la mer Caraïbes par Pterois volitans et P. miles*, scientific report, Université des Antilles et de la Guyane, 2010.

BRÜCKER Pauline and GEMENNE François, "Migrations et déplacements de populations dans un monde à + 4 °C. Scénarios d'évolution et options politiques", Iddri Sciences-po, *Policy Briefs* n° 04/11, December 2011.

COSAERT Patrice, "Les pays touchés par le tsunami: un contexte économique, politique et humain très diversifié", *Les Cahiers d'Outre-Mer*, n° 229, 2005, pp. 89–95.

DUVAT Virginie, "Mondialisation touristique et environnement dans les petites îles tropicales", *Les Cahiers d'Outre-Mer*, n° 236, 2006, pp. 513–39.

FOOD AND AGRICULTURE ORGANIZATION (FAO), *FAO and SIDS, Challenges and Emerging Issues in Agriculture, Forestry and Fisheries*, document prepared by the FAO for the Inter-Regional Conference of Small Island Developing States, Bahamas, 26–30 January 2004.

GOVAN Hugh, Aalbersberg William, Tawake Alifereti and Parks John E., *Locally-Managed Marine Areas: A Guide for Practitioners*, The Locally-Managed Marine Area Network, 2008.

INSTITUT FRANÇAIS DE RECHERCHE POUR L'EXPLOITATION DE LA MER (Ifremer), *Les Ressources minérales marines profondes, synthèse d'une étude prospective à l'horizon 2030*, summary paper from the conclusions of the working group and recommendations of the steering committee of 6 July 2010, Ifremer, 2011.

INSTITUTE FOR RESEARCH AND DEVELOPMENT (IRD), *Exploring tropical environments and societies; The French Polynesian Atolls*, Scientific editors: Loïc Charpy and Philippe Dufour, 2007, http://www.com.univ-mrs.fr/IRD/atollpol/intro.html.

INSTITUTE FOR SUSTAINABLE DEVELOPMENT AND INTERNATIONAL RELATIONS (Iddri) / International Organization for Migration (IOM), *The State of Environmental Migration 2010*, Iddri Sciences-po, *Studies* n° 07/11, December 2011.

SIDS UNIT DIVISION FOR SUSTAINABLE DEVELOPMENT, DEPARTMENT OF ECONOMIC AND SOCIAL AFFAIRS (DESA) and the United Nations Development Programme (UNDP), *SIDS-SIDS Success Stories, an Innovative Partnership in South-South Cooperation*, 2010.

SOLOMON Ranjan, *Tourisme dans les petits Etats insulaires en développement: quelle durabilité?*, Centre Tricontinental (CETRI), Louvain-la-Neuve, 2006.

TOMASETTI Robert J. and HAKEEM Abdul Azeez, *The Role of Resorts on Coral Reef Restoration and Monitoring in the Maldives*, Banyan Tree Marine Lab, Vabbinfaru, Maldives, poster, 11th International Coral Reef Symposium, 2008.

UNESCO, *Embarking on Mauritus Strategy implementation*, Environment and development in coastal regions and in small islands, Unesco, Paris, 2005.

UNESCO, *Islands in a sea of change*, Unesco's intersectoral platform for SIDS, Unesco, Paris, 2009.

UNESCO, *Building island resilience*, Unesco's intersectoral platform for SIDS, Unesco, Paris, 2011.

UNITED NATIONS, *The Impact of Climate Change on the Development Prospects of the Least Developed Countries and Small Island Developing States*, Office of the High Representative for the Least Developed Countries, Landlocked Developing Countries and Small Island Developing States (UN-OHRLLS), 2009.

UNITED NATIONS, *Trends in Sustainable Development: Small Island Developing States (SIDS)*, un, Department of Economic and Social Affairs, Division for Sustainable Development, New York, 2010.

UNITED NATIONS, *Small Island Developing States, Small Islands Big(ger) Stakes*, Office of the High Representative for the Least Developed Countries, Landlocked Developing Countries and Small Island Developing States (UN-OHRLLS), 2011.

UNITED NATIONS ENVIRONMENT PROGRAMME (UNEP), *UNEP and Small Island Developing States: 1994 to 2004 and Future Perspectives*, United Nations Environment Programme, 2004.

UNITED NATIONS ENVIRONMENT PROGRAMME (UNEP), *Seas, Oceans and Small Islands*, *Our Planet*, magazine of the United Nations Environment Programme, vol. 15, n° 1, 2004.

VAN BEUKERING Pieter, Brander Luke, Tompkins Emma and McKenzie Emily, *Valuing the Environment in Small Islands. An Environmental Economics Tool Kit*, Joint Nature Conservation Committee's "Environmental Economics with the Overseas Territories in the Caribbean" (EEWOC) Project, http://www.jncc.gov.uk/page-4065, 2007.

WORLD METEOROLOGICAL ORGANIZATION, *SIDS – Saving Paradise, Ensuring Sustainable Development*, WMO-n° 973, 2005.

WORLD TOURISM ORGANIZATION (WTO), *From Davos to Copenhagen and Beyond: Advancing Tourism's Response to Climate Change*, World Tourism Organization, Madrid, 2009.

VIDEO DOCUMENTARIES

CLUA Éric, *Le Corail à tout prix*, CRISP, 2009.

CLUA Éric, *Petit poisson deviendra grand*, CRISP, 2010.

GOISMIER Pierre, *The Voice of the Islanders*, Nausicaá/Studio K, 2011.

INSIGHTSHARE, *Tofiga O Pili Aau*, Samoa, 2009.

MARCH Briar, *There Once Was an Island: Te Henua e Nnoho*, On The Level Productions, 2010, www.thereoncewasanisland.com.

Organisations mentioned

INTERNATIONAL ORGANISATIONS

Alliance of Small Island Developing States (AOSIS)
www.sidsnet.org/aosis
International organisation representing small islands within the United Nations and in international forums.

Caribbean Environmental Health Institute (CEHI)
www.cehi.org.lc
Based in St. Lucia, this technical institute analyses the impact of human activity on the environment and its consequences on human health and the socioeconomic development of countries in the Caribbean region.

Climate Frontlines – Small Islands and Indigenous Knowledge Section – Unesco
www.climatefrontlines.org
Global platform for indigenous peoples, small islands and vulnerable communities so that their voices and concerns are heard in international debates on climate change.

Global Environment Facility (GEF) Small Grants Program
www.sgpsamoa.ws
Financed by the United Nations Development Programme (UNDP), this programme supports microfinance projects to help local populations adapt to climate change on the islands of Samoa, Niue, Cook and Tokelau.

Global Forum on Oceans, Coasts and Islands
www.globaloceans.org
Organisation created to establish a permanent evaluation and a "lobby" on a global scope and at every level of society so that commitments concerning the ocean environment made at the 2002 World Summit on Sustainable Development in Johannesburg are effectively held.

Global Island Partnership (GLISPA)
www.cbd.int/island/glispa.shtml
Partnership for the implementation of the work programme concerning islands prepared by the members of the Convention on Biological Diversity. This organisation helps to obtain funding for grassroots action, while conserving natural resources for the benefit of the islands' inhabitants.

Indian Ocean Commission (IOC)
www.ioconline.org
Grouping the Comoros, Madagascar, Reunion (France), Seychelles and Mauritius to defend their political, economic and trade interests, this regional body works to promote human development and sustainable environmental management.

Intergovernmental Oceanographic Commission of Unesco (IOC/Unesco)
ioc-unesco.org
Organization dedicated to fostering international cooperation and coordinating ocean research programs in order to improve its management and protection and lessen the risks of marine origin.

International Coral Reef Initiative (ICRI)
icriforum.org
International forum bringing together scientists, private, institutional, and non-government organisations for the preservation of coral reefs. The French Initiative for Coral Reefs (Ifrecor) is the French variant of Icri.

Intersectoral Platform for Small Island Developing States of Unesco
www.unesco.org/en/sids
This international platform of exchanges between small island states coordinates Unesco's contribution to the implementation of the Mauritius Strategy for the Sustainable Development of Small Island Developing States (SIDS).

Local and Indigenous Knowledge Systems Section of Unesco
www.unesco.org/new/en/natural-sciences/priority-areas/links/
The LINKS section of Unesco is responsible for developing the recognition of indigenous knowledge in monitoring global environmental changes and the measures envisaged for adapting to them.

Regional Activity Centre for Specially Protected Areas and Species of the Caribbean (SPAW-RAC)
www.car-spaw-rac.org
Housed in Guadeloupe's national park and under the aegis of the Regional Coordination Unit of the United Nations Environment Programme in Kingston (Jamaica), the SPAW-RAC works on the implementation of the SPAW protocol concerning the protection

of marine and coastal biodiversity in the wider Caribbean region.

Sandwatch Program
www.sandwatch.ca
This network, developed with the support of Unesco, allows students and teachers to monitor and analyse their coastal environments in twenty-five island countries.

Secretariat of the Pacific Community (SPC)
www.spc.int/fr
Comprising twenty-two islands in Oceania, this body provides technical, scientific and strategic aid in the area of sustainable development, through assistance, training and research missions.

University Consortium of Small Island States (UCSIS)
www.unesco.org/en/unitwin
Interuniversity alliance comprising the universities of the South Pacific, the Western Antilles, the American Virgin Islands, Mauritius and Malta. The universities of Las Palmas and Seychelles may join in the future.

NATIONAL INSTITUTIONS

Atmospheric Radiation Measurement (ARM) Program – Climate Research Facility – U.S. Department of Energy
www.arm.gov
American scientific institution responsible to the Department of Energy, which studies climate and sets up observation stations on islands.

Coastal Protection Agency (France)
www.conservatoire-du-littoral.fr
This French public body's objective is to acquire and permanently protect ecologically threatened sections of the nation's shoreline. It notably coordinates the Small Mediterranean Islands initiative (PIM).

The Coral Reef InitiativeS for the Pacific, or CRISP
www.crisponline.info
French initiative for coral reefs of the Pacific financed by the French Fund for the World Environment and the French Development Agency (AFD).

French Marine Protected Areas Agency
www.aires-marines.fr
Public establishment dedicated to the marine environment, which runs the marine protected areas network in mainland France and on the French islands.

French Research Institute for Exploration of the Sea (Ifremer)
www.ifremer.fr
French scientific institute carrying out research on the ocean, whose range of skills covers underwater technology, biodiversity, fisheries and aquaculture, coastal environment, mineral resources, biotechnology and operational oceanography.

Madagascar Institute for Fishing and Marine Science (IHSM)
www.nodc-madagascar.org
Malagasy scientific institute dedicated to training and research in the area of fisheries, aquaculture, and marine and coastal environment. The IHSM conducts a program of raising sea cucumbers with two Belgian universities (the Free University of Brussels and the University of Mons-Hainaut) and the private Madagascar company Holothurie SA.

National Oceanic and Atmospheric Administration (NOAA)
www.noaa.gov
American agency in charge of ocean and atmospheric studies, its mission being to understand and predict marine and atmospheric changes, and to raise public awareness.

Protected Area Network, Palau
palau.chm-cbd.net/protected-area-network
Marine protected area network for the Republic of Palau.

Seamarc – Reefscapers Project
www.reefscapers.com
Environmental consultancy that manages the Reefscapers programme for the raising and reintroduction of coral reefs in the Maldives.

Seychelles Fishing Authority (SFA)
www.sfa.sc
Semi-public organisation for research and development and the management of fishing in the Seychelles.

Seychelles Island Foundation
www.sif.sc
Government organization, which manages nature reserves on the World Heritage List in the Seychelles Islands.

ASSOCIATIONS

Alofa Tuvalu
www.alofatuvalu.tv
French-Tuvalu association responsible for setting up concrete and reproducible campaigns in the Tuvalu archipelago to reduce greenhouse gas emissions. Its projects represent a range of methods for environmental protection.

Chumbe Island Coral Park Ltd. (CHICOP), Zanzibar/Tanzania
www.chumbeisland.com
Marine park offering environmental education programmes and ecotourism.

Conservation International
www.conservation.org
This association is based in the United States but is present in some forty countries. It works for the preservation of marine and terrestrial biodiversity, especially in biodiversity "hot spots", and conducts many island programmes.

Foundation for the Protection of Marine Biodiversity (FoPRoBIM)
www.foprobim.org
Haitian association devoted to protecting the ocean, replanting mangroves, education and management of marine protected areas.

Foundation of South Pacific People (FSP)
www.fspi.org.fj
Based in Fiji and bringing together ten Pacific countries, this organisation coordinates community programmes.

Grenada Education and Development Project (GRENED)
www.grened.org
This association teaches women and children about sustainable development in Grenada in the Caribbean.

International Union for Conservation of Nature (IUCN)
www.iucn.org
International association bringing together a network of over 1,000 government and non-government organisations in some 160 countries. IUCN experts establish a Red List of endangered species. In its role as the official technical advisory body of Unesco, the IUCN evaluates natural site candidates for World Heritage status and monitors them.

"Les Insulaires" Festival
lesinsulaires.com
This festival is meant be a space for exchanges and meetings and a platform for reflection on the future of the Ponant Islands, France.

Locally-Managed Marine Area network (LMMA)
www.lmmanetwork.org
Marine protected area network overseen by local communities in the Pacific and Indian oceans.

Marine Conservation Society Seychelles
www.mcss.sc
Organisation devoted to the preservation of whale sharks and the whole of marine biodiversity in the Seychelles.

Megaptera
www.megaptera.org
Founded in Mayotte, this association is devoted to the observation, awareness of, and protection of marine mammals, dugongs and whale sharks. It organises programmes in Mayotte, Madagascar, the Comoros, Reunion, Djibouti and in Polynesia.

Ocean Futures Society
www.oceanfutures.org
Founded by Jean-Michel Cousteau, this American association encourages awareness of sustainable development and protection of the marine environment. It operates the Amassadors of the Environment programme and is a partner in Fiji Islands Cousteau Resort where the principles of ecotourism are put into practice.

Reef Environmental Education Foundation – Caribbean
www.reef.org
Network of professional and amateur divers who work for the conservation of reefs and are especially

involved in the battle against invasive species in the Carribean.

Reef Check
www.reefcheck.org
A non-profit international organisation, Reef Check is dedicated to the conservation of coral reefs. Its headquarters are in California, but volunteer teams are active in eighty countries, including France.

Sea Level Rise Foundation
www.sealevelrise.blogspot.fr
Organisation dedicated to raising awareness of the impacts of climate change on islands.

Seychelles Hook and Line Fishermen – Fishing Boat Owners Association
seychelles-hookandline-fishermen.org
Fishermen's association that is responsible for the establishment of an eco-label for artisanal fishing that is sustainable and responsible in the Seychelles.

Te Mana o Te Moana
www.temanaotemoana.org
Having as its mission the conservation of the marine environment and raising public awareness, this association notably introduces children to the natural wonders of the Pacific isles.

Trans-Mad' Développement
www.transmad.org
Carrying out development programmes in Madagascar, this association notably supports the establishment of sea cucumber farms in order to preserve the reef and to provide resources for fishermen.

Tuvalu Overview
tuvalu-overview.tv
Based in Tuvalu and in Tokyo, this association attempts to raise awareness about the situation of Tuvalu in the face of climate change. In collaboration with the Hidenori Watanabe Laboratory (Tokyo Metropolitan University), it has set up the project "Build the Future with 10,000 Tuvaluans".

World Wide Fund for Nature (WWF)
wwf.panda.org
International association for the protection of nature in some hundred countries, offering 1,200 conservation programmes. It operates numerous preservation and sustainable development projects on islands.

Nausicaá

A PLACE FOR UNDERSTANDING THE TIES BETWEEN THE OCEAN AND HUMANITY

What are the major environmental issues faced by mankind today? What solutions are being implemented around the world to try to preserve the world's oceans, humanity's common heritage? We must answer these critical questions. Created in 1991, Nausicaá, the Centre National de la Mer at Boulogne-sur-Mer, is not just your ordinary aquarium… Its mission is to educate and raise awareness about mankind's relationship with the Ocean. In this meeting place for all of those interested in the "blue planet", everyone discovers the incredible profusion of life in the Ocean – from coral reefs to abysses, from the high seas to the coasts, including cold seas and mangrove forests. Over 34,000 animals, 46 aquariums, 9 terrariums, soundscapes and light shows combine to make it an unforgettable experience.

Visitors also learn about ocean-related issues, its importance for the planet's equilibrium and changes that are affecting it today. Exhibitions, conferences that make it possible to interact with those involved in the preservation of the marine world internationally, Nausicaá TV…: these are so many keys to understanding the evolution of our environment. Since 2011, Nausicaá has been living in synch with islands thanks to the multimedia project "Islands' Stories" (exhibition, films, books, partnerships with the Alliance of Small Island States…), co-produced with the Mare Nostrum aquarium.

www.nausicaa.fr

WORLD OCEAN NETWORK – RÉSEAU OCÉAN MONDIAL

Aquariums and science centres are in a unique position for raising public awareness. Thus, in 2002, the idea was born to found the World Ocean Network, which gathers together over 450 member organisations and partners in 60 countries around the world, reaching hundreds of millions of visitors. Its mission: to develop a worldwide programme promoting awareness of the Ocean, spreading information about its importance for mankind and encouraging people to take action.

www.worldoceannetwork.org

Mare Nostrum

A NEW WAY TO DISCOVER THE SEA AND TO BETTER UNDERSTAND ITS ISSUES AND THE NEED TO PRESERVE ITS RESOURCES

In keeping with the sustainable development efforts of the Greater Montpellier area, Mare Nostrum is an educational and recreational facility that entertains, while inspiring visitors and raising their awareness about the preservation of marine biodiversity.

Dive in among the wonders of the Mediterranean, follow the ocean currents to challenge the southern Ocean and cross the Roaring Forties, go down into the eerily mysterious abysses, then contemplate the vastness of the ocean before coming back up in the heart of the warm seas and tropical forests, teeming with hundreds of multi-coloured species – that is the amazing voyage that Mare Nostrum offers its visitors.

This "new generation" aquarium uniquely combines the playful, the scientific and the educational, and presents each theme with its appropriate species. It thus proposes a new way to discover the ocean, a total immersion for a unique experience!

In 2011, Mare Nostrum took on an extra dimension, thanks to its first thematic exhibition "Islands' Stories", co-produced with Nausicaá. This exhibition puts special emphasis on the relationship between islanders and their environment. It highlights their creativity and the examples they set in searching solutions for the future.

Through this exhibition, Mare Nostrum is reinforcing its missions of environmental education, conservation incentives and management of marine resources.

JEAN-PIERRE MOURE
President of the Greater Montpellier Authority

www.aquariummarenostrum.fr

Acknowledgments

Our most sincere thanks go to:

RONNY JUMEAU, ambassador of the Seychelles to the United Nations
AFELEE FALEMA PITA, ambassador of Tuvalu to the United Nations
They convinced us that it was urgent to devote a book to islands and give a voice to their inhabitants.

For their precious contribution to this work, we would also like to thank:
LUCIE AH-KONG, professional fisherwoman, attached to the artisanal fishing port of Mahé, Seychelles

BRENDA ANDIMIGNON, in charge of educational programmes at the Seychelles Ministry of the Environment, Seychelles

FABRICE BERNARD, European and International delegate to the Coastal Protection Agency, France

LOUIS BRIGAND, island specialist, teacher-researcher in geography at the University of Western Brittany (UBO), France

LINDSAY CHONG SENG, biologist specialised in biodiversity, former director of the Seychelles Island Foundation

ERIC CLUA, programme coordinator in research and technology, representing the Ministry of Higher Education and Research to the French High Commissioner of French Polynesia, former coordinator of the programme CRISP "Coral Reef InitiativeS for the Pacific"

CLAUDE COLIN, former attaché at the French Embassy in the Seychelles

JEAN-MICHEL COUSTEAU, president of the Ocean Futures Society, United States

JOE DINGWALL, president of Seychelles Hook and Line Fishermen – Fishing Boat Owners Association

BERTY HOAREAU, professional fisherwoman, member of the Seychelles Hook and Line Fishermen – Fishing Boat Owners Association

JEANNETTE LARUE, environmental action coordinator for the Ministry of Education, Seychelles

CHRISTOPHE LEFEBVRE, delegate to the European and International section of the Marine Protected Areas Agency and president of the French Committee of the International Union for Conservation of Nature (IUCN), France

FRANCK MAZÉAS, programme coordinator at the Department of the Environment, Development and Housing (DEAL) and the French Coral Reef Initiative (Ifrecor), Guadeloupe

RICHARD MURPHY, scientific director of the Ocean Futures Society, United States

DOUGLAS NAKASHIMA, head of Unesco's Small Islands and Indigenous Knowledge Section

ROLPH PAYET, Minister of Environment, Seychelles

SIBYLLE RIEDMILLER, director of the Chumbe Island Coral Park, Zanzibar

JAN ROBINSON, head of the department of research at the Seychelles Fishing Authority (SFA)

LYNNE ROEDER, information officer for the Atmospheric Radiation Measurement (ARM) Climate Research Facility, United States

DAVID ROWAT, director of the Marine Conservation Society of Seychelles

SUSIE SAITALA KOFE, jurist, president of the Alofa Tuvalu Association

AKE STANDLEY, president of the Women's Committee of Vaiusu, Samoa

HANS THULSTRUP, programme specialist for the Intersectoral Platform for Small Island Developing States (SIDS), Unesco

MICHEL VÉLY, president of the association Megaptera, Mayotte

WENDY WATSON-WRIGHT, assistant director-general and executive secretary of the Intergovernmental Oceanographic Commission, of Unesco

JEAN WIENER, director of FoProBiM, Haiti

DESSIMA WILLIAMS, Grenada's ambassador to the United Nations, former president of the Alliance of Small Island States

as well as:

TREASSY ARRISOL, Seychelles Hook and Line Fishermen – Fishing Boat Owners Association

GARETT BENEST, Conversations with the Earth

RICHARD CRICHTON, KEVIN PETRINI and OLLIE REUPENA, UNDP Samoa Multi Country Office

SHUICHI ENDO and MASAE ITO, NPO Tuvalu Overview

CÉCILE GASPAR, president of Te Mana o Te Moana, French Polynesia

FANNY HÉROS, Alofa Tuvalu

KHALISSA IKHLEF, Unesco's Small Islands and Indigenous Knowledge Section

SÉBASTIEN RENOU, France's Coastal Protection Agency

FRANCIS STAUB, International Coral Reef Initiative (ICRI)

CAROLINE VIEUX, Global Island Partnership (GLISPA)

The authors would also like to warmly thank ALL OF THE NAUSICAÁ CREW, *particularly* CHISTOPHE PERRIN, ALINE COUSIN-KLAWINSKI *and* ISABELLE LEGRAND.

Éditions Actes Sud, Philippe Vallette, Christine Causse and Alexis Rosenfeld thank for her maritime complicity ISABELLE AUTISSIER, sailor and writer, member of the advisory board of the French Australs and Antarctic Islands.

PHOTOGRAPHIC CREDITS

All photos are by Alexis Rosenfeld, except for those mentioned below.
Pages 42, 49, 51, 92 (at top) and 118 (at top): Michel Renaudeau
Pages 43 and 48: Hervé Tiberghien
Pages 52–53: Ulla Lohmann
Page 58 (at top and at lower left): Gilles Martin-Raget
Page 61: Kjeld Ibsen
Pages 62, 66 (at right), 67 and 220 (the two photos in the middle): FoProBIm
Pages 66 (at left), 100–01, 144, 167, 193 (at left), 199 (at bottom), 208–09, 220 (at bottom), 226–27, 232 and 239: Pascal Kobeh
Pages 133, 161 (at right) and 193 (at right): ARM Climate Research Facility
Pages 148 (at top left) and 162 (at bottom): CRISP
Pages 160 (at right) and 161 (at left): Franck Mazeas
Page 162 (at top): Ocean Futures
Page 162 (in the center): Chumbe Island Coral Park
Pages 176–77: Gary Braasch
Pages 180 and 187: Shuuichi Endou / Tuvalu Overview
Page 249: Mare Nostrum

EDITORIAL COORDINATION
Anne Bresson-Lucas and Aïté Bresson

GRAPHIC DESIGN
Christel Fontes and Anne Ambellan for the English version

MAPS
Jean-Pierre Magnier

PRODUCTION
Camille Desproges

PROOFREADING
Christine Schultz-Touge

PHOTOENGRAVING
IGS

Printed and bound in August 2012
by Gibert-Clarey printers in Chambray-lès-Tours, France
for Actes Sud - Le Méjan, place Nina-Berberova, 13200 Arles, France

French legal registration of copyright: 1st edition: October 2012
ISBN Actes Sud 978-2-330-01008-9

www.actes-sud.fr